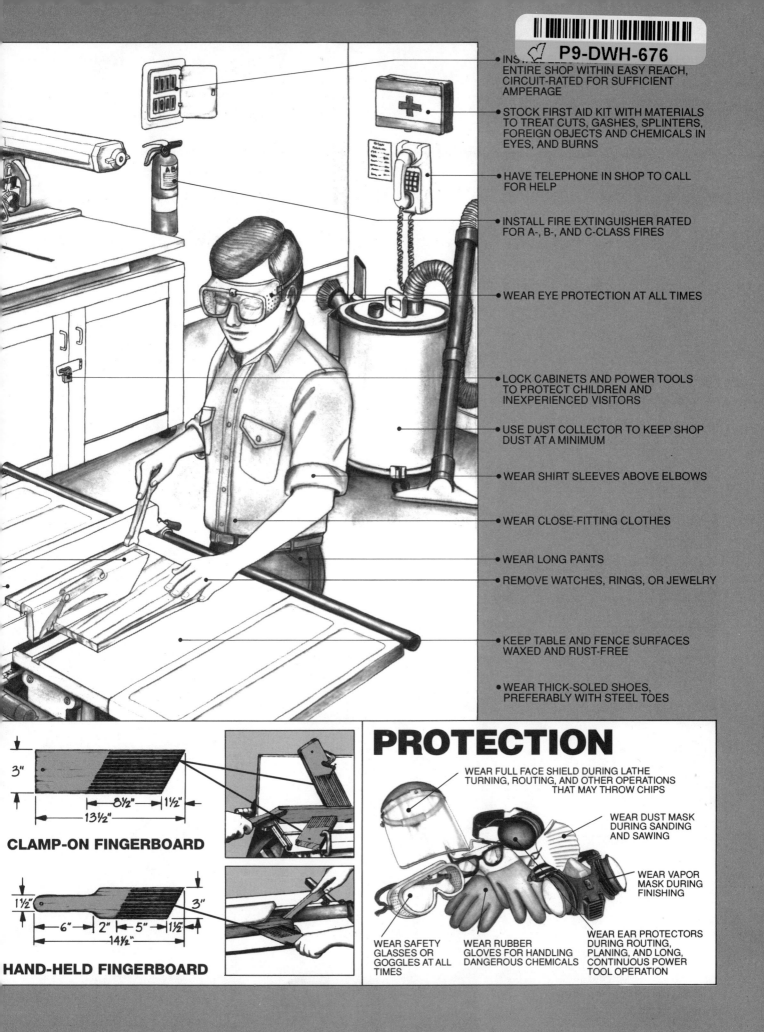

- INSTALL [...] ENTIRE SHOP WITHIN EASY REACH, CIRCUIT-RATED FOR SUFFICIENT AMPERAGE

- STOCK FIRST AID KIT WITH MATERIALS TO TREAT CUTS, GASHES, SPLINTERS, FOREIGN OBJECTS AND CHEMICALS IN EYES, AND BURNS

- HAVE TELEPHONE IN SHOP TO CALL FOR HELP

- INSTALL FIRE EXTINGUISHER RATED FOR A-, B-, AND C-CLASS FIRES

- WEAR EYE PROTECTION AT ALL TIMES

- LOCK CABINETS AND POWER TOOLS TO PROTECT CHILDREN AND INEXPERIENCED VISITORS

- USE DUST COLLECTOR TO KEEP SHOP DUST AT A MINIMUM

- WEAR SHIRT SLEEVES ABOVE ELBOWS

- WEAR CLOSE-FITTING CLOTHES

- WEAR LONG PANTS

- REMOVE WATCHES, RINGS, OR JEWELRY

- KEEP TABLE AND FENCE SURFACES WAXED AND RUST-FREE

- WEAR THICK-SOLED SHOES, PREFERABLY WITH STEEL TOES

CLAMP-ON FINGERBOARD

3"
8½" 1½"
13½"

HAND-HELD FINGERBOARD

1½"
6" 2" 5" 1½"
14½"
3"

PROTECTION

WEAR FULL FACE SHIELD DURING LATHE TURNING, ROUTING, AND OTHER OPERATIONS THAT MAY THROW CHIPS

WEAR DUST MASK DURING SANDING AND SAWING

WEAR VAPOR MASK DURING FINISHING

WEAR SAFETY GLASSES OR GOGGLES AT ALL TIMES

WEAR RUBBER GLOVES FOR HANDLING DANGEROUS CHEMICALS

WEAR EAR PROTECTORS DURING ROUTING, PLANING, AND LONG, CONTINUOUS POWER TOOL OPERATION

THE WORKSHOP COMPANION™

JOINING WOOD

TECHNIQUES FOR BETTER WOODWORKING

by Nick Engler

Rodale Press
Emmaus, Pennsylvania

Printed in the United States of America on acid-free ∞, recycled paper ♲

If you have any questions or comments concerning this book, please write:
Rodale Press
Book Reader Service
33 East Minor Street
Emmaus, PA 18098

About the Author: Nick Engler is an experienced woodworker, writer, and teacher. For many years, he was a luthier making traditional American musical instruments before he founded *Hands On!* magazine. Today, he contributes to other how-to magazines and has published over 20 books on the wood arts. He teaches woodworking at the University of Cincinnati.

Series Editor: Jeff Day
Editors: Roger Yepsen
         Kenneth Burton
Copy Editor: Sarah Dunn
Graphic Designer: Linda Watts
Graphic Artists: Mary Jane Favorite
                 Chris Walendzak
Photographer: Karen Callahan
Cover Photographer: Mitch Mandel
Proofreader: Hue Park
Typesetting by Computer Typography, Huber Heights, Ohio
Interior and endpaper illustrations by Mary Jane Favorite
Produced by Bookworks, Inc., West Milton, Ohio

Library of Congress Cataloging-in-Publication Data

Engler, Nick.
    Joining wood/by Nick Engler.
        p.   cm. — (The workshop companion)
    Includes index.
    ISBN 0–87596–121–5   hardcover
    1. Woodwork.   2. Timber joints.   3. Joinery.   I. Title
    II. Series.
    TT185.E54   1992
    684'.08—dc20   91–36032
                                              CIP

2   4   6   8   10   9   7   5   3   1   hardcover

The author and editors who compiled this book have tried to make all the contents as accurate and as correct as possible. Plans, illustrations, photographs, and text have all been carefully checked and cross-checked. However, due to the variability of local conditions, construction materials, personal skill, and so on, neither the author nor Rodale Press assumes any responsibility for any injuries suffered, or for damages or other losses incurred that result from the material presented herein. All instructions and plans should be carefully studied and clearly understood before beginning construction.

Special Thanks to:

Sotheby Parke Bernet Inc.
New York, New York

Wertz Hardware
West Milton, Ohio

CONTENTS

TECHNIQUES

PROJECTS

Techniques

1

A JOINERY PRIMER

Think back to your first woodworking experience. Chances are that this fateful deed, which set you on the road to becoming a woodworker, involved joining two or more pieces of wood. My first act of craftsmanship was to nail several wooden blocks to my parents' coffee table. The satisfaction of solidly joining one board to another encouraged me to explore other areas of woodworking. (That very evening I learned how to cut a switch.)

Joinery, after all, is the heart of woodworking. Project design, wood selection and preparation, sanding, and finishing are important, too. But we spend most of our shop time cutting large boards into little pieces, then assembling those pieces with the hope of making something useful. More than any other woodworking skill, joinery determines the utility and durability of the project. This could be why early woodworkers referred to themselves as "joiners."

Joinery, unfortunately, is also one of the most misunderstood subjects in woodworking. It's easy to see why. Open any book on woodworking and you'll see dozens, maybe hundreds of ways to join one board to another. Each one seems more intricate than the last. With so many joints to choose from, how can you possibly determine which is best for a particular job?

It needn't be so confusing. All those complex joints are just variations on a few simple themes.

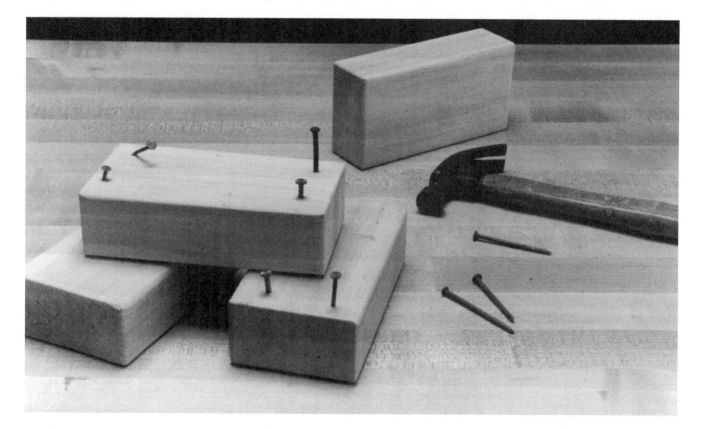

TYPES OF JOINTS

THREE BASIC OPERATIONS

Boards can be joined in three different ways:

■ *Fitting* joins the mating surfaces of the parts with no gaps or openings. The boards are cut to fit one another. These cuts can be as simple as those in a butt joint or as intricate as the tails and pins of a dovetail joint.

■ *Gluing* bonds two boards with a chemical adhesive, such as animal hide glue, aliphatic resin (yellow) glue, or epoxy.

■ *Fastening* secures one board to another with wood or metal fasteners, such as pegs, nails, and screws.

To make most wood joints, you must combine two or more of these basic operations. For example, you might fit a simple butt joint and reinforce it with nails. Dovetail joints are typically fitted and glued. And a few joints, such as a pegged mortise and tenon, combine all three activities — fitting, gluing, *and* fastening. (*SEE FIGURE 1-1.*)

FOUR WAYS TO FIT

Of these three operations, however, fitting is the most essential. You can join wood without glue or nails, but not without fitting. Even a simple butt joint requires that you cut one board to fit flush against the surface of another. Gluing and fastening are important — and I'll refer to them from time to time — but fitting is the essence of joinery. Most of this text focuses on how to *fit* four basic types of joints (*SEE FIGURE 1-2*):

■ *Simple joints,* such as dadoes and rabbets, require only a few simple cuts to assemble two parts.

■ *Reinforced joints* use a secondary piece of wood, such as a dowel or spline, to strengthen the joint between two or more principal parts.

■ *Mortise-and-tenon joints* have one part that is bored or recessed to hold a second part, and are mostly used to join the parts of a *frame*.

■ *Interlocking joints* use multiple cuts to increase the adjoining surface area, and usually join the parts of a *box*.

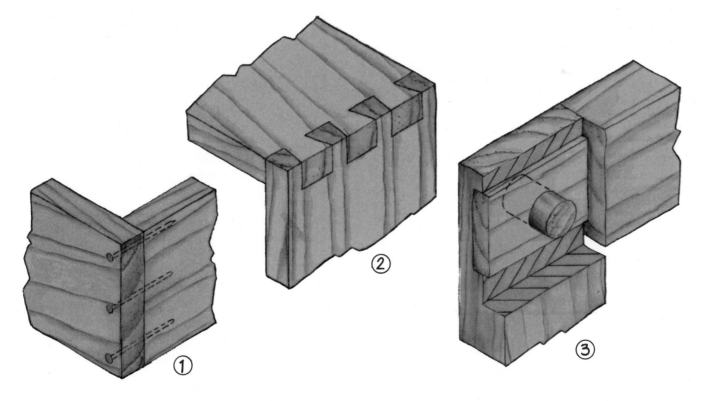

1-1 Most woodworking joints combine two joining operations — either fitting and fastening, as with the nailed butt joint (1), or fitting and gluing, as with the dovetail joint (2). Some combine all three, such as the pegged mortise-and-tenon joint (3) — it's fitted, fastened, *and* glued. Note that all of these joints require some degree of *fitting*. Just as joinery is the heart of woodworking, fitting is the heart of joinery.

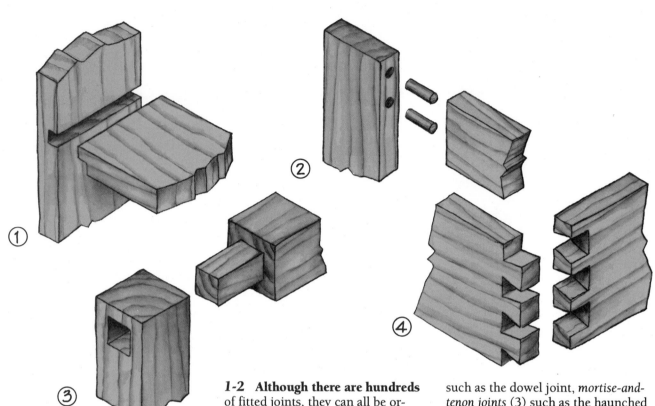

1-2 Although there are hundreds of fitted joints, they can all be organized into four categories — *simple joints* (1) such as the rabbet-and-dado joint, *reinforced joints* (2) such as the dowel joint, *mortise-and-tenon joints* (3) such as the haunched mortise and tenon, and *interlocking joints* (4) such as the through-dovetail joint.

THE PURPOSE OF JOINERY

Now that you know the basic types of joinery, how do you choose the right joint for a particular woodworking job? Consider that every joint must fulfill two important requirements:

■ It must *support the load* of the other parts and any external weights or forces that might be applied to the completed project.

■ It must *let the wood move* as it expands and contracts with changes in temperature and humidity.

And if the joint is to be glued or fastened, as most are, there is a third requirement:

■ It must *provide a suitable gluing surface or anchor* for a fastener.

Use whichever joint best fulfills these requirements.

SUPPORT THE LOAD

The parts of a woodworking project are elements of what engineers call a "stress system." Each joint must withstand a certain amount of stress pushing or pulling at the members of the joint. This stress comes from many different sources. It could be external (coming from outside the structure); for example, when you sit on a chair, your weight stresses the chair joints. If you scoot the chair across the floor, the friction between the floor and the chair legs creates stress. Or the stress could be an internal factor, inherent to the structure. The tension in a woven seat, for example, stresses the joints between the rails and the legs. Even the weight of the individual chair parts, no matter how small or light they may be, is an internal stress to be reckoned with.

There are four types of stress, categorized by the direction of the force relative to the joint (*SEE FIGURE 1-3*):

■ *Tension* pulls the members of a joint apart.

■ *Compression* squeezes the members together.

■ *Shear* pushes the members in opposite directions. The lines of force are parallel, but not aligned as they are with tension and compression.

■ *Racking* (or bending) rotates the members around one another.

Even before they've been glued or fastened, fitted joints resist one or more types of stress. (*See Figure 1-4.*) After they're assembled, they resist all types to a greater or lesser degree. When choosing a joint, try to pick one that will withstand the anticipated stress without glue or fasteners. That way, if the glue bond or the hardware fails, the joint will stay together.

FOR YOUR INFORMATION

Of the four types of stress, racking is the most destructive. A racking force bends the members of a joint like levers. A lever, as you know, will move a heavy object when you apply a relatively small force — the force is multiplied by the pivoting action of the lever. For this reason, a small amount of racking will pop a joint that might otherwise withstand large amounts of tension, compression, or shear.

For most woodworking projects, however, you must do more than pick a joint or two. You must design an entire *system* of joints — this is what a structure is. To build a structure, you must determine not only the types of joints in it but also their size and location relative to each other. This isn't difficult; it just takes some thought. There are a few simple commonsense methods for designing a strong, durable structure:

■ Use larger joints and structural members. This distributes the load over a larger area and larger mass. (*See Figure 1-5.*)

■ Use smaller members, but more of them. This too increases the area and mass that supports the load. (*See Figure 1-6.*)

■ Triangulate the members. Rearrange the structural members or add new members, braces, glue joints, or fasteners to create structural triangles. When a triangle is fastened at all three corners, it's very rigid. This is why engineers triangulate bridges and roof trusses. (*See Figure 1-7.*)

■ Orient the wood grain properly; wood is always strongest parallel to the grain. A tenon or dovetail cut across the grain will soon break.

■ Increase the glue surface in a joint by making the fitted surfaces more intricate. (*See Figure 1-8.*)

■ Increase the size or the number of fasteners.

■ Use both glue *and* fasteners.

BUTT JOINT
RESISTS COMPRESSION
ONLY

MORTISE & TENON
RESISTS COMPRESSION,
SHEAR, & RACKING

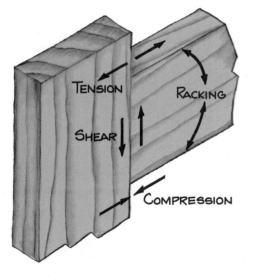

1-3 Four types of stress may tear a wood joint apart — *tension, compression, shear,* and *racking.* Of these, racking is the most destructive.

1-4 Even before a butt joint is glued or fastened, it will withstand compression, but any amount of tension, shear, or racking will pull it apart. A mortise-and-tenon joint, on the other hand, will resist compression, shear, and racking. Only tension can pull it apart before it's secured.

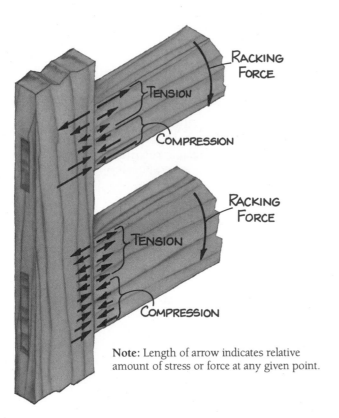

RACKING FORCE

TENSION

COMPRESSION

RACKING FORCE

TENSION

COMPRESSION

Note: Length of arrow indicates relative amount of stress or force at any given point.

1-5 The racking force applied to both of these mortise-and-tenon joints is equal. But on the large mortise and tenon (*bottom*), the load is distributed over a larger area and more mass. The stress at any one point in the joint is a good deal less than that on the smaller mortise and tenon (*top*).

1-6 You don't have to use massive structural members or joints to support a large load. On this Shaker rocker, the load is distributed over many small, round mortise-and-tenon joints. The chair's frame and joinery appear very delicate, yet it has survived constant use for almost two centuries.

1-7 Structural triangles don't all have to look like roof trusses. On a table, the upper part of the leg and the apron form a hidden triangle that keeps the structure rigid. On a board-and-batten door, the nails form triangles that keep the door square.

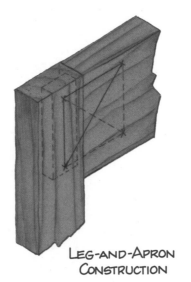

LEG-AND-APRON CONSTRUCTION

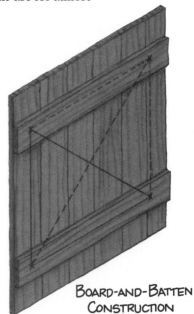

BOARD-AND-BATTEN CONSTRUCTION

1-8 The adjoining members of both the butt joint (*left*) and the box joint (*right*) are precisely the same size. However, the fitted fingers of the box joint offer more gluing surface than the flat surfaces of the butt joint. Consequently, the box joint is much stronger.

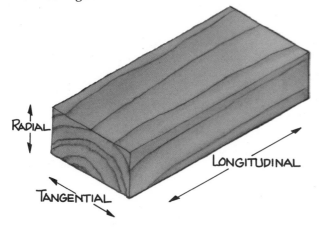

1-9 Wood moves in three different planes — *longitudinal,* or parallel to the wood grain, *radial,* or perpendicular to the annual rings, and *tangential,* or tangent to the annual rings. Wood is fairly stable longitudinally — it will only shrink or swell .1 percent of its length when originally cut. However, it's unstable radially and tangentially. Furthermore, the tangential movement in most woods is about twice the radial movement. Radial movement averages 4 percent (of the original cut dimension) and tangential movement averages 8 percent.

LET THE WOOD MOVE

Wood shrinks and swells with changes in the relative humidity (the amount of moisture in the air relative to the temperature). When the relative humidity goes up, the wood absorbs some of this moisture and swells. When the relative humidity goes down, the wood loses moisture and shrinks. Since the average relative humidity in much of the world is lower in the winter than it is in the summer, wood tends to shrink each winter and swell each summer.

> ## FOR YOUR INFORMATION
> **O**n the average, the moisture content of wood changes 1 percent for every 5 percent change in the relative humidity.

This movement, although it may seem slight, is extremely important to woodworkers. To see why, try this experiment: Using waterproof glue, attach a small, narrow board to a wide one so the grain directions are perpendicular. Set this assembly outside on a rainy day and the boards will separate, despite the waterproof glue. As the wide board expands in the opposite direction of the narrow one, the joint is subjected to an increasing amount of shear stress. Eventually, it breaks. More joints fail from wood movement due to changes in moisture than from abuse and neglect. You must take this movement into account and accommodate it in your joinery.

Wood moves in three planes, and it moves differently in each plane. (*SEE FIGURE 1-9.*) All three types of motion are relative to the direction of the wood grain and annual rings:

■ *Longitudinal* movement is parallel to the wood grain.

■ *Radial movement* is perpendicular to the annual rings *and* to the wood grain.

■ *Tangential* movement is tangent to the annual rings and perpendicular to the wood grain.

Wood is fairly stable longitudinally. An 8-foot-long spruce board will shrink less than $1/16$ inch along its entire length, from the time it's cut "green" (and about as saturated with moisture as it will ever be) to the time it's dried to 7 or 8 percent moisture content (dry enough for cabinetmaking and furnituremaking). Consequently, most woodworkers treat wood as if it were motionless along the grain.

Across the grain, it's a different story: Some woods may move up to ¼ inch for every 1 foot of width or thickness. Furthermore, there is a big difference between radial and tangential movements. Most wood species will shrink or swell about twice as much tangent to the annual rings as perpendicular to them. "Tangential/Radial Movement of Common Wood Species" on the facing page compares the movement of several species along these different planes. As the ratio of tangential movement to radial movement becomes greater, it becomes increasingly important that you properly align the tangential and radial planes of adjoining parts.

The disparity between radial and tangential movement causes yet another type of movement to consider as you choose the joinery. Depending on how a board is sawed from a tree, it may *deform* as it shrinks and swells. For example, if the annual rings run from side to side in a square table leg, the leg may become rectangular as the wood shrinks faster from side to side than from front to back. If the rings run diagonally from corner to corner, the leg may shrink to a diamond shape. A round dowel becomes an oval as the wood shrinks, and a flat board cups in the opposite direction of the annual rings. (*SEE FIGURE 1-10.*) Sometimes you can use joinery to help control this deformation; other times you must simply plan for it.

This is a lot to think about. Joinery would be far simpler if wood were the relatively stable building material that many beginning woodworkers take it to be. But it's attention to details such as wood movement that marks the difference between a true craftsman and a novice. To properly join wood, not only must you plan a joint system that allows the wood to move, but you must also "read" the wood figure as you make each joint. Study each board, then orient the grain and the rings so the anticipated movement creates the least possible stress on the joint.

There are several simple joinery techniques that help reduce stress and/or control deformation caused by wood movement. Use those techniques that apply to the structure of your project.

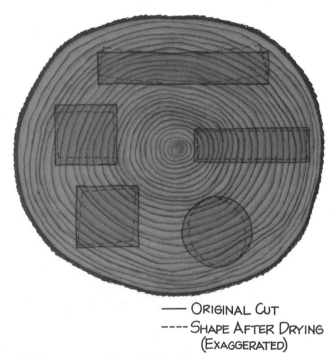

—— ORIGINAL CUT
---- SHAPE AFTER DRYING
(EXAGGERATED)

1-10 **Because the radial and** tangential movement of wood is uneven, boards tend to deform as they go through an annual moisture cycle. The way a board will deform depends on how it is cut from the tree.

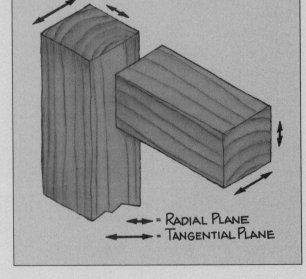

TRY THIS TRICK

To help visualize the wood movement in a joint, sketch the boards as they will be assembled, showing the wood grain and annual rings. Mark each board with a small arrow to indicate radial movement and a large arrow to indicate tangential movement. Try to orient the wood figure so the large arrows are all parallel.

◄—► = RADIAL PLANE
◄——► = TANGENTIAL PLANE

Orient the wood figure to make each part as stable as possible. Since the longitudinal plane of a board is the most stable, align this plane with the longest dimension (the length). Align the radial plane with the next longest dimension (the width), and the tangential plane with the shortest dimension (the thickness). This may not always be possible, since most boards are "plain-sawn" from logs so the *tangential*

plane is aligned with the width. If the alignment of the tangential and radial planes is critical, you may have to pay a premium price for "quarter-sawn" lumber, in which the *radial* plane is aligned with the width. Or you can rip a board into narrow strips and glue it back together with the rings properly aligned. (SEE FIGURE 1-11.)

1-11 Usually, the larger the board, the more critical it is that the longitudinal, radial, and tangential planes all be aligned for maximum stability. This is why furniture-makers glue up "butcher block" tabletops from narrow strips. Notice that each strip has been turned so the annual rings run top to bottom. The radial plane of each strip is aligned with the width of the table-top. The tangential plane — the most unstable dimension of each strip — is aligned with the thick-ness, where stability matters least.

TANGENTIAL/RADIAL MOVEMENT OF COMMON WOOD SPECIES

SPECIES	TANGENTIAL*	RADIAL*	T/R RATIO
Ash, white	7.8%	4.9%	1.6 to 1
Birch, yellow	9.2%	7.2%	1.3 to 1
Cedar, aromatic	5.2%	3.3%	1.6 to 1
Cedar, western red	5.0%	2.4%	2.1 to 1
Cherry	7.1%	3.7%	1.9 to 1
Elm, American	9.5%	4.2%	2.3 to 1
Fir, Douglas	7.6%	4.1%	1.9 to 1
Mahogany	5.1%	3.7%	1.4 to 1
Maple, hard	9.9%	4.8%	2.1 to 1
Maple, soft	8.2%	4.0%	2.1 to 1
Oak, red	8.9%	4.2%	2.1 to 1
Oak, white	10.5%	5.6%	1.9 to 1
Pine, white	6.1%	2.1%	2.9 to 1
Pine, yellow	6.2%	3.9%	1.6 to 1
Poplar, yellow	8.2%	4.6%	1.8 to 1
Redwood	4.9%	2.2%	2.2 to 1
Spruce, Sitka	7.5%	4.3%	1.7 to 1
Teak	4.0%	2.2%	1.8 to 1
Walnut	7.8%	5.5%	1.4 to 1

*Percentage of shrinkage from when wood is first cut (green) to after it is kiln dried.

Orient the wood figure so the parts move in unison.
Whenever possible, join the boards so the wood
swells and shrinks in the same direction. When the
wood grain must cross at right angles, align the *tangential* planes. (*SEE FIGURES 1-12 AND 1-13.*)

Cut large boards into smaller parts. When you must
glue or otherwise fasten two boards with opposing
wood grain, make sure they are as narrow as possible
without compromising the strength of the structure.
(*SEE FIGURES 1-14 AND 1-15.*)

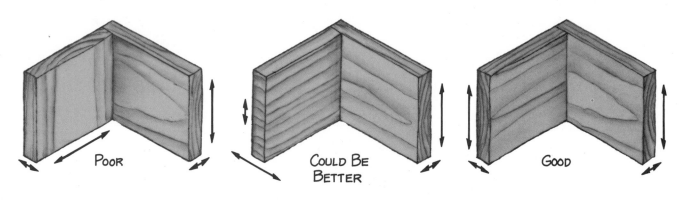

1-12 On the corner butt joint
shown at the left, both the wood
grain and the annual rings are opposed to one another. The joint will
soon fail. On the middle joint, the
wood grain is aligned, but the annual rings are not — the tangential
planes are perpendicular to one
another. This joint will fail too,
though not as quickly as the first.
On the joint at the right, both the
wood grain and the annual rings are
properly aligned. This joint will last
for a long time.

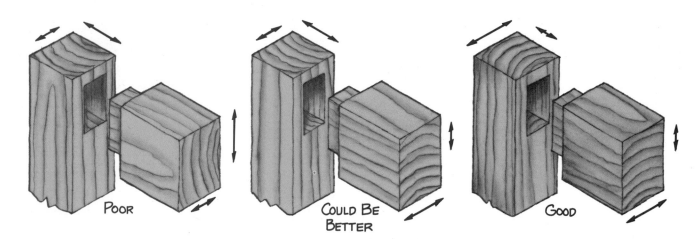

1-13 The wood grain on all three
of these mortise-and-tenon joints is
properly aligned. But on the joint
at the left, the tangential planes are
directly opposed on the broadest possible surface — where the cheeks of
the tenon meet the sides of the mortise. This greatly diminishes the useful life of the joint. On the joint in
the middle, the planes are in some-
what better alignment. The tenon
moves radially at right angles to the
tangential movement of the mortise.
But the joint at the right shows the
best possible arrangement — the
tenon moves radially at right angles
to the radial movement of the mortise, and the tangential planes are
aligned.

FOR BEST RESULTS

As a rule of thumb, most craftsmen limit the width of lap joints and mortise-and-tenon joints (where the wood grains of the members must be glued perpendicular to one another) to *3 inches* when the *tangential* planes can be aligned, and less if they can't be.

Use "floating" joints to let the wood move. When you must join a large board to a structure and cannot cut it into smaller pieces, do *not* glue it in place. Instead, let it float in a groove or dado, free to expand and contract. *(SEE FIGURE 1-16.)* You can also make floating joints with screws and bolts. Cut a slot for the shank of the screw or bolt, allowing the wood to expand and contract around it. *(SEE FIGURE 1-17.)*

1-14 This antique spice cabinet was built in the late nineteenth century, when boards up to 24 inches wide were commonly available. However, the craftsman who built it chose to make the back from narrow boards, since he had to attach them at right angles to the shelves. This has prevented the back from buckling as it expanded and contracted for almost a century.

1-15 This apron will be joined to a table leg with a mortise-and-tenon joint. Like all such joints, this presents a dilemma — the mortise grain is perpendicular to the tenon grain, so the two parts move in different planes, stressing the joint. The wider the mortise and tenon, the more the parts move and the more critical this problem becomes. To alleviate some of the stress that a single wide joint might generate, the tenon on the end of this apron has been "split" into two narrower ones, each less than 3 inches wide. Instead of one wide tenon expanding and contracting in a single large mortise, there are two smaller tenons, each moving only half as much in its own mortise — and only generating half the stress. And because the gluing surface has not been greatly diminished, this split mortise-and-tenon joint is still very strong.

1-16   Traditional frame-and-
panel construction, such as these
cabinet doors, employs floating
joints. The panels expand and contract in grooves cut in the inside
edges of the rails and stiles.

1-17   The shank of this round-
head screw rests in a slot, allowing
the wide board to expand and contract around it. When making floating joints for screws and bolts, cut
the slot with the long direction
parallel to the direction of the wood
movement. Drive the screw snug in
the slot, but not so tight that it
restricts movement.

TRY THIS TRICK

Use small nails for floating joints when
applying a small molding, as many old-time
woodworkers did. The grain direction of a molding is often perpendicular to that of the board to
which it's applied. If you secure the molding with
brads, these tiny nails will bend slightly as the
wooden parts expand and contract.

Avoid wood that may deform and stress the joint. As
mentioned previously, wood not only moves, but
also may change shape. Study the wood figure to
anticipate how a board might deform. If this deformation will create stress in the joinery, use another
board. *(SEE FIGURE 1-18.)*

If possible, control the deformation. Wood *will*
expand and contract no matter what you do. If you
restrict the movement, you will make matters worse.
Wood will deform, too, and though this can't be

stopped, it can often be controlled. For example, a
well-placed batten, brace, or screw can control cup-
ping. *(SEE FIGURE 1-19.)* Sometimes, you don't need anything at all — just align the wood figure properly in
the joint to restrict the deformation. *(SEE FIGURE 1-20.)*

FOR BEST RESULTS

After designing a joint system that allows
the wood to expand and contract and carefully
aligning the wood figure in each joint, there is
one more thing you must do to relieve the stress
due to wood movement — apply a finish. A good
finish slows the release and absorption of moisture, and prevents the wood from shrinking or
swelling too quickly. This, in turn, protects the
wood from radical changes in relative humidity
that often occur several times a week — sometimes several times a day! The wood movement is
slower and gentler, and the joinery lasts longer.

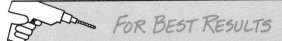

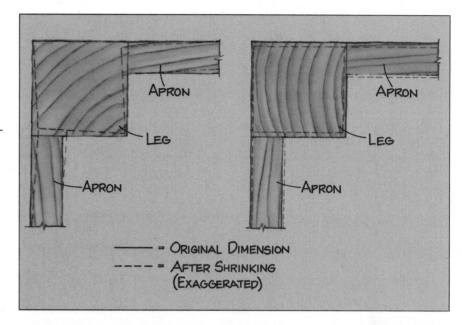

1-18 Because the annual rings run diagonally through the leg on the left, the wood will expand or contract to a diamond shape. This will pull the aprons out of alignment so they are no longer square to one another. If the aprons were attached at the other end, all the joints in the leg-and-apron assembly would be stressed. Not so with the leg on the right. Because the rings run side to side, the wood will expand or contract to form a rectangle. Although the wood does deform, the aprons remain properly aligned.

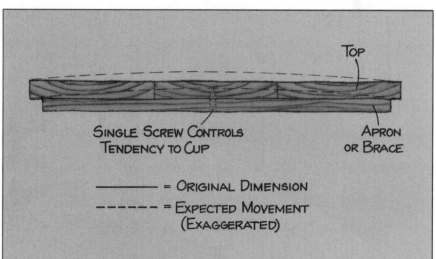

1-19 If you glue up a wide tabletop (*not* a butcher block) from narrower boards, turn the annual rings to curve *up*. If the board cups, the top will tend to rise in the middle. You can control this tendency by fastening the tabletop to the apron near the middle of the table. This leaves the sides free to expand and contract.

1-20 When assembling a box or drawer, turn the boards so the annual rings curve *out,* as shown on the right. The boards' natural tendency to cup will keep the corner joints tight at the edges. If the annual rings curve in, as they do on the left, the joints may pull apart at the edges.

PROVIDE A SUITABLE GLUING SURFACE OR ANCHOR

As mentioned previously, the most obvious thing you can do to increase the strength of a glue joint is to increase the gluing surface. However, this isn't always as simple as it sounds. There are four different ways to glue one board to another, and some are stronger than others. *(SEE FIGURE 1-21.)* In descending order of strength, you can glue wood:

■ Long grain to long grain, with the grain parallel
■ Long grain to long grain, with the grain perpendicular
■ Long grain to end grain
■ End grain to end grain

If you increase the gluing surface by fitting the joint differently, don't sacrifice long-grain surface for end-grain surface — that may actually weaken the joint. Nor do you always want to increase the long-grain-to-long-grain surface where the wood grains are perpendicular. If these surfaces become too broad,

the wood movement might pop the joint. Consider other ways to expand the surface — make several small joints, or reinforce the glue bond with dowels or splines.

TRY THIS TRICK

To increase the strength of end-grain glue joints, paint the end grain with a thin coat of glue and wait about half an hour. Apply another coat of glue — this time, apply it as thick as you would normally — and clamp the parts together. The first thin coat prevents the end grain from absorbing the second coat, resulting in an even and continuous glue bond. However, don't rely on end-grain glue joints alone when strength is important.

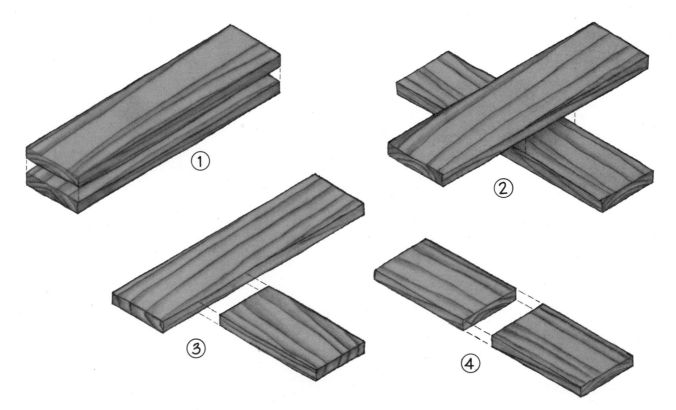

1-21 The strongest glue joint you can make is long grain to long grain with the grain parallel (1). Long grain to long grain with the grain perpendicular (2) is almost as strong, but the members of the joint move in opposite directions. This weakens the glue bond. A long-grain-to-end-grain joint (3) has some strength, but the end grain absorbs much of the glue and the adhesive film isn't continuous; consequently, the bond is weak. In an end-grain-to-end-grain joint (4), this problem is aggravated. Since both boards absorb the glue, the bond is even weaker.

You might also consider whether you need to increase the gluing surface at all. Providing a *suitable* gluing surface does not necessarily mean a large gluing surface. You can build strong, durable projects without oversize, intricate joints. *(See Figure 1-22.)* There are several other important things you can do to ensure a good glue joint:

■ *Make the glue surfaces as smooth as possible.* A thin, even, continuous film of glue is essential for a strong joint. Rough surfaces make the film uneven and create voids.

■ *Fit the surfaces properly.* The surfaces must fit together without any gaps. Gaps create an uneven glue film and weaken the bond. At the same time, the fit must not be too tight. A tight fit will squeeze the glue from between the boards, leaving a weak, "starved" joint.

■ *Clean the surfaces.* Give the glue surfaces a light sanding with very fine sandpaper before applying the glue. This removes any foreign materials. It also helps the glue to soak in and form what chemists call an "interface" — an integral bond between the adhesive and the wood. As you sand, be careful not to round-over adjoining surfaces.

The considerations are similar if you're making a fastened joint. The first thing that comes to mind when you must provide a suitable anchor for a nail or screw is to beef up the wood around it. But this isn't the only thing you can do to strengthen a fastened joint. As with a glue joint, you must consider the orientation of the wood grain. Nails and screws hold better when you drive them *through* the long grain. They may pull out or even split the wood if you drive them into the end grain. You can also:

■ Use more, smaller fasteners instead of a few large ones.

■ Drive fasteners at angles to one another, locking the parts together. *(See Figure 1-23.)*

■ Use square-shanked nails or ring-shanked nails instead of ordinary nails with round, smooth shanks. The large surface area of square-shanks and the protrusions on ring-shanks help to hold the nail in the wood.

■ If you must drive screws or nails into end grain, use fasteners that are as long as practical. The extra length helps them to hold tight.

1-22 You don't need beefy, intricate joinery to make strong glue joints. This reproduction of a Shaker lap desk is made from thin stock (many parts are only ³/₃₂ inch thick) so it is as light as possible. With the exception of the dovetail joints at the corners, the joinery consists of simple butts, rabbets, and grooves. But the assembled desk is sound and solid.

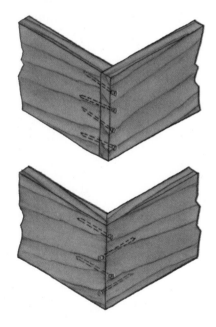

1-23 Here are two ways you might lock boards together with nails. In the butt joint (*top*), the nails are driven at slight angles, alternating right and left with each nail. In the miter joint (*bottom*), the nails are driven at right angles to one another. In both cases, the opposing angles of the nails make the joint difficult to pull apart.

The Value of Simplicity

MAKING YOUR FINAL CHOICE

Even after carefully reviewing the requirements, you'll likely find that there are two or more good candidates for each joinery job. How do you choose between them? There is a brilliantly simple rule of thumb that many experienced woodworkers use to cut through this Gordian knot of joinery. But before I let you in on this secret, let me tell you a brief story.

Several years ago, I wrote a piece on reproducing a Chippendale block-front desk. The original was built in 1765 in Newport, Rhode Island — possibly by the master colonial cabinetmaker/woodcarver, Edmund Townsend. The desk had just sold at auction for over half a million dollars. (*SEE FIGURE 1-24.*)

As I researched the desk, I ran across an old magazine article by an accomplished woodworker who had built a similar piece. His account of the project was daunting. "Complex" was too mild a word to describe the joinery. The bracket feet, for example, were assembled with double-blind mitered dovetails! I've never met a woodworker who managed to complete a double-blind mitered dovetail in his lifetime,

but I understand the effort required is in the same order of magnitude as the Lewis and Clark expedition.

Next, I visited the head craftsman of the restoration shop at Sotheby's — the outfit that had sold the desk. In interviewing him, I found he had replaced one of the bracket feet. I was awed. I was in the presence of a woodworking deity! What advice did this Olympian have for mere mortals faced with the task of making double-blind mitered dovetails?

"Oh, you read *that* article," he said with a laugh. Then he went on to explain, "Townsend was in the cabinetmaking business, and like most businessmen, he was concerned with production. He didn't have time to spend on over-engineered joinery."

So how did the great Edmund Townsend join the bracket feet on his half-million-dollar desk?

"A simple miter and a glue block."

So here's the secret: When choosing among the myriad woodworking joints, remember that *plain often does just as well as fancy.* In many cases, it will do better.

1-24 Chippendale blockfront desks made by the Townsend family of Newport, Rhode Island, are among the finest and most valuable pieces of eighteenth-century American furniture. Although these desks are elegantly crafted, the joinery is surprisingly simple.

2

SELECTING TOOLS AND PREPARING MATERIALS

In this age of computerized power tools and gee-whiz accessories, we too often overlook wonderfully uncomplicated tools and techniques. Take the scratch awl, for example. Without a computer chip to guide it, or even a switch to turn it on, would you have guessed what an unsurpassed layout tool it is? Have you ever taken the time to acquire the simple knack for using a hand plane competently? Or have you stopped to

think how many joints you can make with an ordinary table saw and a few well-chosen blades?

We also forget what a fickle material wood is. Modern-day "manufactured" woods — plywood, particleboard, and laminates — have lured us into a false sense of security. We don't think twice about pulling a surfaced board from a lumberyard bin and incorporating it into a project with little preparation. We just

assume the board is as stable as the simulated wood that surrounds us. We ignore what our great-grandfathers knew too well — raw wood often hides a tortured past. Unless this hidden strain is exposed and exorcised, your project can be ruined.

As mentioned, wood joinery is simple and obvious. Before you can cut and fit a good joint, you must wake up to these simple wonders and obvious dangers.

JOINERY TOOLS

Like any woodworking operation, joinery requires specific tools. Most of these are common woodworking tools. They are not hard to find, expensive to buy, or difficult to use. However, to make precise, well-fitted joints, the tools should be precise and well made.

LAYOUT TOOLS

The most important joinery tools are those tools required to measure and lay out joints. *(SEE FIGURE 2-1.)* If you have only a limited amount of money to invest in woodworking equipment, purchase top-notch layout tools and skimp on everything else. You can cut better joints with a good square and a mediocre table saw than you can with a mediocre square and the world's greatest saw.

To lay out most joints, you need:

- A *scratch awl* or a *marking knife* to scribe layout lines on the wood
- A *marking gauge* to scribe lines parallel to one surface of a board
- A *compass* to scribe arcs and circles
- Small and large *rules* to make most measurements
- *Calipers* to make small, precise measurements
- Small and large *squares* to measure 90-degree angles
- A *combination square* to measure 45- and 90-degree angles
- *Drafting triangles* to measure 30-, 45-, and 60-degree angles
- A *protractor* to measure "odd" angles (other than 30, 45, 60, or 90 degrees)
- A *sliding T-bevel* to transfer these odd angles to the wood

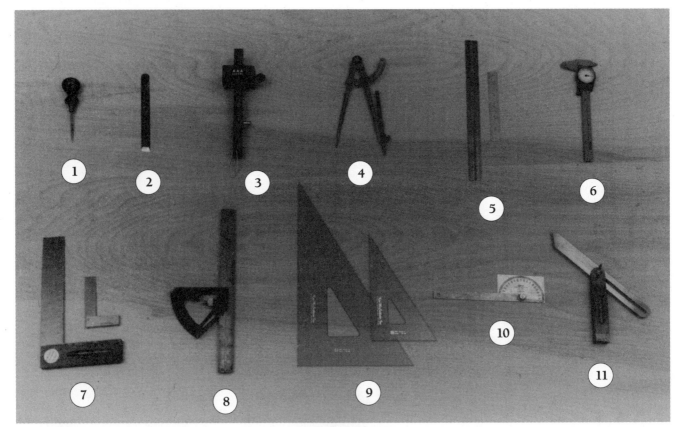

2-1 Before you can cut a joint, you must lay it out. Different joints require different layout tools, so you must keep a selection of measuring and marking devices in your tool box: a *scratch awl* (1), a *marking knife* (2), a *marking gauge* (3), a *compass* (4), small and large *rules* (5), *calipers* (6), small and large *squares* (7), a *combination square* (8), *drafting triangles* (9), a *protractor* (10), and a *sliding T-bevel* (11).

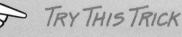

TRY THIS TRICK

To make sure a square is indeed square, hold the square's base against the edge of a board and scribe a straight line along one side of the straightedge. Flip the square over and draw a second line next to the first, using the same edge as a guide. The two lines should be parallel. If they aren't, your square isn't.

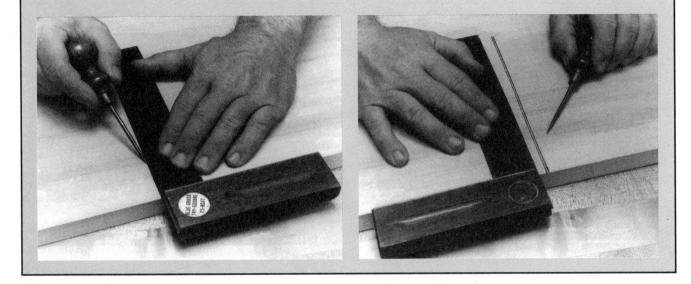

You're probably familiar with the rule, compass, square, and other measuring tools. But the marking tools — the scratch awl, marking knife, and marking gauge — may take some getting used to. Most beginning woodworkers use a pencil to lay out cuts. This is a poor choice — pencils are untrustworthy marking tools. As the tip grows dull, the line becomes broader and reduces the accuracy of the cut.

A *scribed* layout line — a line drawn with a sharp metal point — remains crisp and even from the beginning to the end. In addition, the point severs the wood grain as you scribe the line. This helps prevent tearout and chipping when you make the cut. The resulting cut not only is more accurate; it's cleaner. (*SEE FIGURE 2-2.*)

Unfortunately, a marking tool with a metal point is harder to use than a pencil until you acquire the knack. First of all, you must properly sharpen the tool. File the points of scratch awls and marking gauges to look like tiny knives. (*SEE FIGURE 2-3.*) The points should *cut* the wood grain, not tear it. When you scribe a line, press down *lightly* on the tool as you draw it across the wood. If you apply too much pressure, the point will dig in and follow the wood grain rather than cutting a straight line. Make several passes, cutting the line a little deeper with each pass. Continue until the line is as deep as you want it.

2-2 Scribing a layout line will help prevent the blade or cutter from tearing the wood when you make the cut. The dado on the left was laid out in pencil, and the one on the right with an awl. The sides of the left dado are torn and chipped, while those on the right are clean.

TRY THIS TRICK

If you have trouble seeing a scribed line, dust it with a little of the powdered blue chalk carpenters use in snap lines. When you're done, simply wipe the chalk off the wood with a damp rag. Don't use the red chalk; it's harder to remove and may interfere with some finishes.

2-3 Most scratch awls and marking gauges come with round points, as shown on the right. These scratch the wood, tearing the grain. File and hone the points to make tiny two-edged blades, as shown on the left. A blade cuts the grain, leaving a crisper line.

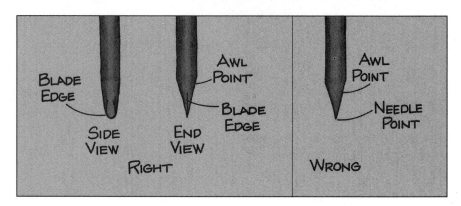

HAND TOOLS

Even if you prefer to use power tools, you'll need a few good hand tools for making joints. There are times when it's quicker to cut a joint by hand than it is to spend the time needed to set up a power tool. Also, there are a few woodworking operations that you can perform better with hand tools, and a few more that you can perform *only* with hand tools.

We won't discuss *all* the useful hand tools just yet; I'll introduce some of these later, as we need them. Right now, let's cover the essentials. (*See Figure 2-4.*) At a minimum, you need:

■ A set of *paring chisels* — ¼ inch, ½ inch, and ¾ inch — to remove waste stock from mortises, notches, and other joints

■ A small *mallet* to drive the chisels

■ A *jack plane* to smooth surfaces and trim large areas of long grain

■ A *block plane* to trim end grain and small areas of long grain

■ A small *hammer* to drive nails

■ A small *nail punch* to set nails

■ A *dovetail saw* for making small, fine cuts

Selecting hand tools is largely a matter of personal preference. You want something that "fits your hand" — you'll do better work and more of it with a comfortable, well-balanced tool than with one that feels awkward. Here are some additional tips on selecting chisels, planes, and saws:

For fine joinery, use *beveled-edge paring* chisels, not *framing* chisels (also called "firmer" chisels). The difference is subtle, but important. Paring chisels have thinner blades with sloped edges, while framing chisels are beefier and have square edges. (*See Figure 2-5.*) These larger chisels are made for carpentry work and cutting large joints. Paring chisels are designed to handle medium-size and small jobs. The thin blades and beveled edges let you cut in tight corners. Make sure you purchase chisels that are designed to be struck by a mallet — not all paring chisels are.

When fitting a joint, you often need to remove small amounts of stock from one or more surfaces until the parts mate properly. There is no tool that will do this better than a hand plane. Get both a block plane for small jobs and a jack plane for large jobs.

When selecting a plane, don't be lured by sexy looks and a high price tag. A plane is a simple tool, and the price makes little difference in how it performs. A medium-quality plane, when properly tuned, will do just as well as the more expensive models.

There are two important steps to tuning a plane. First, sharpen the plane iron so the cutting edge is razor sharp, perfectly straight, and reasonably square to the sides. To maintain a straight edge when sharpening the iron, use a *honing guide* to hold it at a fixed angle to the sharpening stone. *(SEE FIGURE 2-6.)* Second, hone the sole of the plane perfectly flat. If it isn't flat, the plane won't cut cleanly or evenly. *(SEE FIGURE 2-7.)*

When reassembling the plane, position the cap iron (if the plane has one) so the leading edge is $1/16$ inch or less from the cutting edge of the plane iron. If necessary, file the cap iron so there are no gaps between it and the plane iron. Retract the iron into the plane housing, then advance it very slowly. (If you have a metal plane, turn the depth-of-cut screw. If you have a wooden plane, tap the iron with a·mallet.) Stop adjusting when the plane begins to cut paper-thin curls of wood. If necessary, move the iron from side to side until the cutting edge is parallel with the sole.

When choosing a dovetail saw, consider a Japanese *dozuki* saw. *(SEE FIGURE 2-8.)* Unlike European and American saws, the dozuki cuts on the *pull* stroke, making it easier to control. The pull-cut action also

allows the saw maker to use a thinner blade with finer teeth. As a result, the dozuki leaves a narrower kerf and finer cut than Western saws. There is a trade-off, however. Dozuki saws are more expensive than Western dovetail saws, and the blades are more fragile.

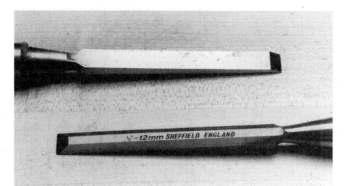

2-5 **A paring chisel (*bottom*) is** designed for versatility and maneuverability. The thin blade and beveled edges let you reach into small slots and tiny corners. The framing chisel (*top*) is not as versatile, but the thick blade and square edges make it better suited for heavy work. Both have their place in your shop, but the paring chisel is more useful for fine joinery work.

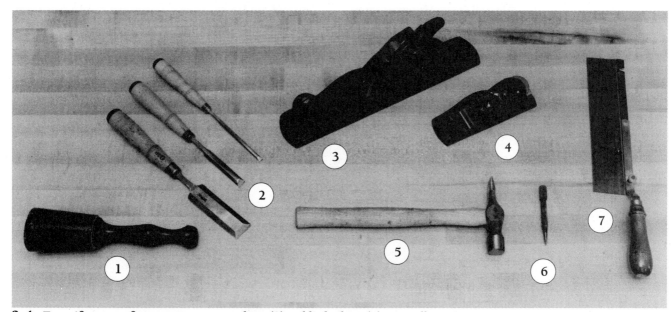

2-4 **Even if you prefer to use** power tools, you'll need a few hand tools for joinery work: a small *mallet* (1), a set of *paring chisels* (2), a *jack plane* (3), a *block plane* (4), a small *hammer* (5), a *nail punch* (6), and a *dovetail saw* (7).

2-6 The sharpness of a plane
iron depends on four things — the
straightness of the cutting edge, the
accuracy with which you hone the
bevel or "face" of the iron, how flat
you hone the back, and how well
you polish both the face and the
back. To maintain a straight edge
and an accurate face, hold the iron
in a *honing guide*. Unless the cutting
edge is deeply nicked, start with a
medium grit (such as a soft Arkansas
stone) and finish with a fine grit
(hard Arkansas). Remove the iron
from the jig and hone the back flat,
progressing through the same grits.
Finally, polish both the face and the
back with buffing compound and
a strop, or with an extremely fine
stone. Both the face and the back
should shine like a mirror.

2-7 To flatten the sole of a metal
plane, you must make a hone. On
a jointer, flatten the face of a block
of hardwood that's about 6 inches
longer and wider than the plane. To
this block, attach a sheet of 220-grit
wet/dry silicon carbide sandpaper
using a spray adhesive. (If the block
is very big, use several sheets of
sandpaper, butting — but *not* lapping — the edges.) Hone the plane
sole on this block. When the sole is
flat, replace the 220-grit sandpaper
with 320-grit. Work your way up
through progressively finer grits
until the sole is flat and smooth. If
you wish, polish the sole with buffing compound on a large sheet of
fine leather.

2-8 For most woodworkers, a
Japanese *dozuki* dovetail saw (*left*)
cuts faster and smoother than its
Western counterpart (*right*). Unfortunately, it costs more and the blade
requires careful maintenance.

POWER TOOLS

By and large, contemporary woodworkers rely on power tools for most of their joinery work. Although these require more set-up time than hand tools, power tools will perform most woodworking tasks faster and easier. And for woodworkers who can't afford the time and practice it requires to master hand tools, power tools do the work more accurately.

There are dozens of power tools and hundreds of accessories for joinery work. But you can make most joints with just a few versatile machines:

■ A *jointer* to true up boards in preparation for joining them

■ A *table saw* or *radial arm saw* for butt and miter cuts

■ A *dado cutter* for cutting rabbets and dadoes on the table saw and radial arm saw

■ A *router* for cutting rabbets, dadoes, dovetails, and mortises

■ A *router table* to hold the router when cutting small stock

■ A *hand-held drill* to bore screw holes and dowel holes

■ A *drill press* to bore dowel holes and mortises

■ A *mortising attachment* to bore mortises on the drill press

Some of the machines on this list are redundant, and you may not need them all. For example, if you prefer to cut dadoes and rabbets with a router, you don't need a dado cutter for your power saw. Or if

you'd rather cut mortises with a router or a drill press, why buy a mortising attachment? As with hand tools, your choice of power tools is a personal preference.

When choosing between power tools, however, you should be aware of their advantages and disadvantages. For example, woodworkers often debate the relative merits of table saws and radial arm saws. If you have a shop with limited space (as most of us do), which one should you choose? It's easier to make crosscuts on a radial arm saw. And since you make more crosscuts than any other joinery cut, a radial arm saw could save you time and trouble. However, this machine is more difficult to align than a table saw, and it goes out of alignment easier. Many woodworkers grow tired of checking the alignment before every critical cut, and trade the ease of the radial arm saw for the dependable accuracy of the table saw.

There is also a divided opinion on whether a router or a dado cutter accessory makes better rabbets and dadoes. A router cuts smoother than a dado cutter, and the bottom of the cut is perfectly flat. With a dado cutter, the sides and the bottom may be slightly ragged. (*See Figure 2-9.*) On the other hand, it requires several passes to rout a deep dado, while a dado cutter will remove a large amount of stock in one pass.

If you opt for a dado cutter, you have two more choices — a stacked cutter or a wobble cutter. (*See Figure 2-10.*) The stacked cutter is made up of several different blades — two ⅛-inch-thick outside blades or

2-9 The smoother the surface of the joint, the better it will fit. The smooth surfaces also make a better glue joint. This is why some woodworkers prefer to use a router (*right*) to cut dadoes, rather than a dado cutter (*left*).

2-10 A stacked dado cutter (*left*) is easier to set up and is more stable for heavy-duty work. However, a wobble dado cutter (*right*) is more versatile.

cutters and several inside blades or *chippers*. Chippers come in widths of 1/16 inch, 1/8 inch, and 1/4 inch. To adjust the width of cut, make a sandwich of cutters and chippers, adding or subtracting chippers until the stack is the right width. The wobble cutter is a single blade between two tapered bushings. The bushings hold the blade at a slight angle on the arbor so the blade wobbles right and left as it spins. To adjust the width of cut, rotate the bushings. This increases or decreases the sideways wobble.

The advantage of a wobble cutter is that it will make a cut of any width within a certain range (usually 1/8 inch to 13/16 inch). A stacked cutter will only cut in 1/16-inch increments. To make an odd-sized cut, you have to either add shims between the chippers or make several passes. On the other hand, because the tip of a wobble cutter follows an arc, the bottom of the dado cut is slightly curved. This isn't noticeable in narrow dadoes, but it may be a problem in wide ones. Also, a wobble cutter requires more set-up time — you may have to readjust the position of the bushings several times before the cut is the right width. And a stacked dado cutter is more stable, especially for heavy use. The bushings on a wobble dado can slip.

Finally, there are different arguments for making mortises with a drill press, router, or mortising accessory. Perhaps the quickest way to make a mortise is with a drill press. Simply drill a line of overlapping holes, then true up the sides and ends with a chisel. If you have several mortises to make, it's easier to use a router. Rout a groove or dado for each mortise, then square the ends with a chisel. This, however, requires more set-up time than a drill press. If you cut lots of mortises, you may want to use a mortising accessory. (*SEE FIGURE 2-11.*) This drill press attachment enables you to drill square holes. To make a mortise, simply cut a series of overlapping square holes. There's no need to clean up the ends or sides with a chisel. The trade-off is that a mortising accessory requires careful alignment and maintenance, much more so than either the drill press or the router.

PREPARING THE WOOD

No matter what joint you make or what tools you use to make it, the first step is always to cut and joint the boards straight and true.

As a tree grows, several things may happen that cause the wood to deform when it's sawed into boards. If it grows in an unsheltered area, the tree will buttress itself against the prevailing winds; if it grows on a hillside, it will brace itself against the slope. Either

way, one part of the trunk will be under tension, and the other under compression. The result is called *reaction wood*. When the sawyer cuts a board from this trunk, he partially relieves some of the internal stress, and the board warps, bows, or twists.

Other things can happen to the wood as it's dried and stored. If a board dries too fast or isn't stacked properly on a drying rack, it may deform. A board might also deform if it isn't stacked properly after drying, especially after several changes in humidity. Even if a board is cut from a tree that grows straight as an arrow, and it is handled with care as it travels from the sawyer to you, it may still warp, twist, or bow naturally, depending on how it was cut from the log.

2-11 A mortising attachment enables you to bore square holes with a drill press. A *hollow chisel* (1) cuts the flat sides of the holes, while a spiral *drill bit* (2) cuts the bottom and clears the wood chips. Most mortising attachments also come with a *hold-down* (3) to keep the stock from raising up when you retract the drill bit. For tips on how to set up and use a mortising attachment, see "Using a Mortiser" on page 69.

The point is, by the time you get the wood, it's a minor miracle if the board is still straight and square. You must prepare the board for joinery by "truing" the wood — making it straight and square again.

Lumberyards will partially prepare a board for you by throwing it through a planer and surfacing it on two sides. If you're trying to make fine fitted joints, this may do more harm than good. The feed rollers on a typical planer flatten the wood as it passes under a cutter, temporarily removing the cup or warp. But the wood springs back to its deformed shape once it exits the planer.

Instead, you should joint, then plane, the wood. First cut the rough lumber into smaller, more manageable sizes. Many woodworkers "rough cut" all the major parts in a project from rough lumber, sawing each part slightly longer and wider than its final dimensions. This helps detect any reaction wood and relieve any internal stresses that aren't already apparent. Joint two *adjacent* sides — a face and an edge — of each board, making both surfaces perfectly flat and perpendicular to each other. Surface the remaining rough face on a planer, bringing it to its final thickness. Rip the board to within 1/32 inch of its final width, then joint the sawed edge, removing the last bit of stock. The board should be perfectly rectangular. (*SEE FIGURES 2-12 THROUGH 2-15.*)

> ### FOR BEST RESULTS
>
> **W**hen you first purchase lumber, bring it into your shop and let it sit for several weeks before you use it. This will give the moisture content of each board a chance to reach equilibrium with its new environment. If you cut a board while its moisture content is unstable, the wood may expand or contract unevenly. This will ruin the fit of the joints, and may distort the project.

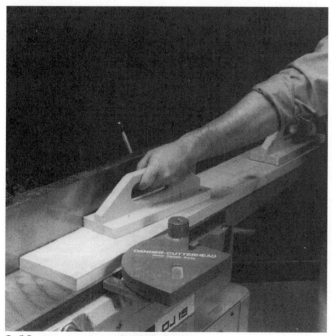

2-12 To prepare a board, first joint the face flat. Inspect the board to see if it's cupped or bowed, then joint it with the concave face *down*. This way, the board will be more stable on the jointer. Next, joint an edge. Inspect the board for crooking, and joint it with the crook *down*. As you cut the edge, hold the jointed face firmly against the fence. When you've finished, both the face and the edge should be flat and straight, and square to one another.

2-13 After jointing one face and one edge, plane the remaining rough face to reduce the board to its final thickness. Use calipers to measure this thickness at several places along the length of the board. The faces should be parallel.

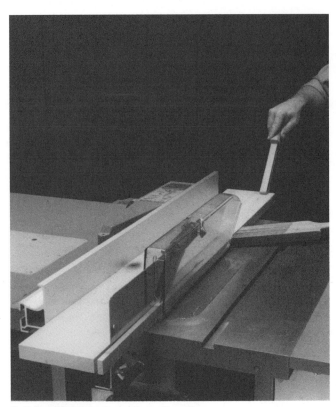

2-14 With the board surfaced on three sides, rip it to within ¹/₃₂ inch of its final thickness on a table saw or radial arm saw. Keep the jointed edge against the fence as you cut.

2-15 Finally, cut the board to its final width by jointing the sawed edge. When you've finished, the edges and the faces should be parallel to one another, and each surface should be square to the adjacent surfaces.

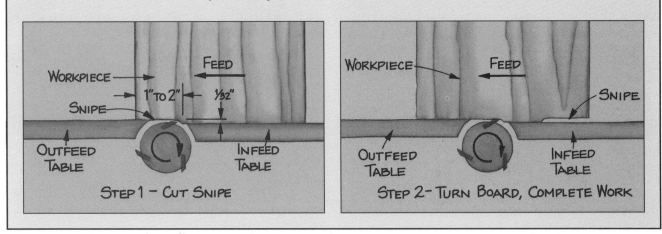

TRY THIS TRICK

Although a jointer is designed to plane long grain — faces and edges — you can use it to joint end grain, if necessary. To do this safely, the board must be wide enough to be stable when resting on its end — at least 10 inches wide. Adjust the depth of cut to ¹/₃₂ inch or less. Feed the board into the knives, jointing the first 1 or 2 inches, which makes a tiny "snipe." Turn the board around and complete the cut. The snipe will prevent the grain from tearing out at the end of the cut.

WORKPIECE   FEED

SNIPE   1" TO 2"   ¹/₃₂"

OUTFEED TABLE   INFEED TABLE

STEP 1 – CUT SNIPE

WORKPIECE   FEED

SNIPE

OUTFEED TABLE   INFEED TABLE

STEP 2 – TURN BOARD, COMPLETE WORK

3

SIMPLE JOINTS

The seemingly endless variety of fitted joints can be daunting to a woodworker. On some, the mated surfaces are so complex that they fit together more like a puzzle than a joint. Your anxiety rapidly dissipates, however, when you realize that much of this complexity is an illusion.

Pick a joint — *any* joint in this book — and study the instructions for how to make it. You'll see that most steps involve simple, familiar woodworking operations. A few joints require that you repeat a simple operation several times, but no matter how complex the joint may look, it's made up of simple elements. There are, in fact, *no* complex joints — just layer upon layer of simplicity.

FIVE CUTS

If you have any remaining doubts about how simple and straightforward wood joinery really is, consider this: There are only five joinery cuts! *Every* fitted joint is made with these:

■ A *butt cut* involves a sawed end, edge, or face that is square to the adjoining surfaces.

■ A *miter cut* leaves a sawed surface at an angle other than 90 degrees to one or more of the adjoining surfaces.

■ A *rabbet cut* makes an L-shaped notch in an arris, or edge, of the board. The bottom and side of the rabbet are usually square to one another.

■ A *dado cut* creates a U-shaped channel in one surface. Like a rabbet, the bottom and the sides of a dado are usually square.

■ A *hole* or "round mortise" is a cylindrical cavity bored into the wood. Holes can be drilled at any angle.

When making these five cuts, you can saw or drill

BASIC WOODWORKING CUTS

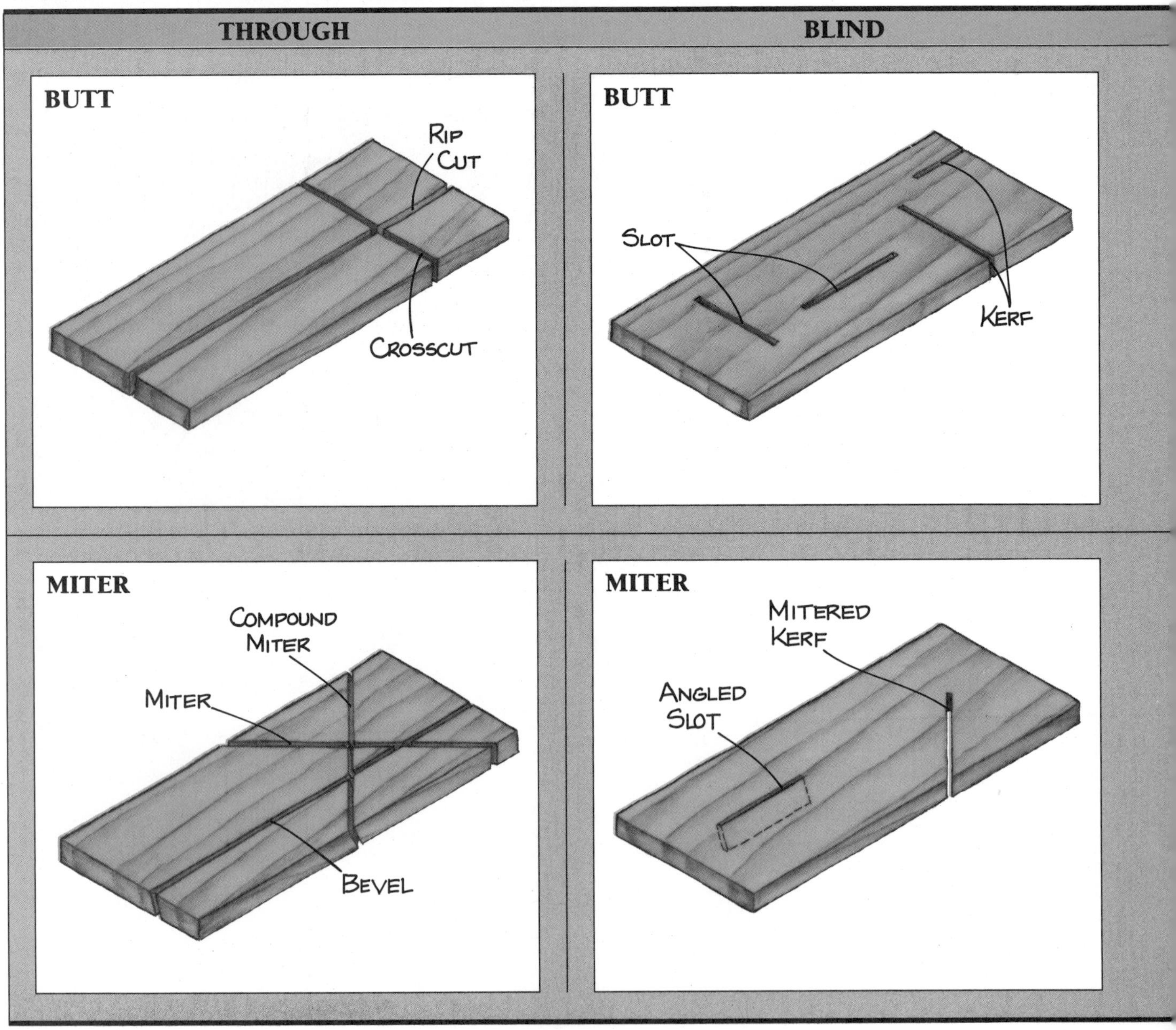

THROUGH	BLIND

BUTT

RIP CUT
CROSSCUT

BUTT

SLOT
KERF

MITER

COMPOUND MITER
MITER
BEVEL

MITER

MITERED KERF
ANGLED SLOT

completely *through* the board, or you can halt partway through the cut, making it *blind* or *stopped*. When a cut is blind, its *length* is limited (like a blind alley). A blind rabbet is closed at one end; a double-blind dado is closed at both ends. "Stopped" refers to the *depth* of the cut and usually applies to holes. A stopped hole has a bottom; it doesn't run through the board.

Every woodworking joint, no matter how complex it might appear, is composed of these simple cuts. For example, a lap joint is made by fitting two dadoes to one another. The mortise in a mortise-and-tenon joint is a double-blind, stopped dado; the tenon is formed from a butt cut (to cut the end of the tenon square) and two or more rabbet cuts. A dowel joint is made of several butt cuts and stopped holes. The trick to making a well-fitted joint is not in making difficult cuts, but in making very simple cuts precisely and in the proper sequence.

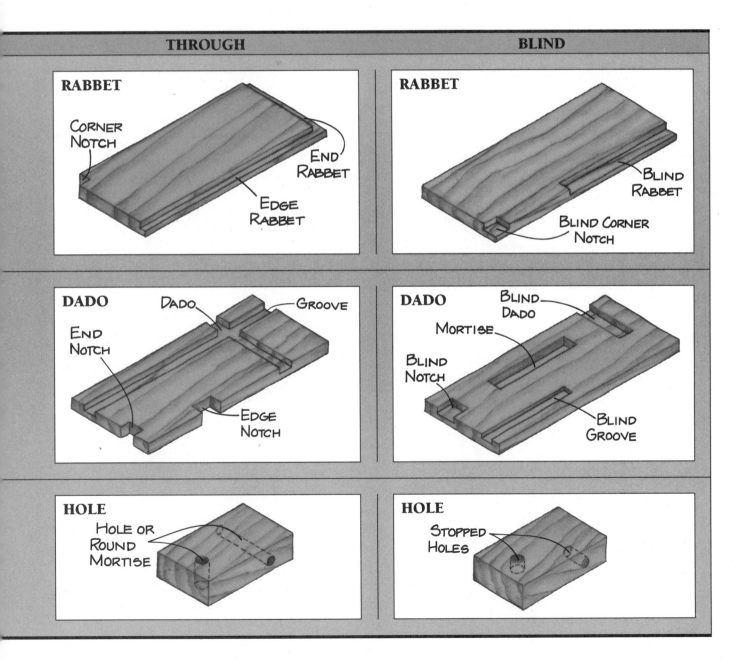

MAKING BUTT CUTS

When making a butt cut — or any joinery cut for that matter — the first step is to check the alignment of the tool. The saw blade *must* be perpendicular to the saw table. *(SEE FIGURES 3-1 AND 3-2.)* In addition, when making a cross cut (on a table saw), the miter gauge must be perpendicular to the saw blade. For a rip cut, the fence or guide must be parallel to the blade. Use squares, drafting triangles, or rules to check these alignments.

After checking the alignments, position a board on the saw. With the saw turned off, advance the board until it touches the blade. Check that the layout lines on the board are properly aligned with the blade teeth. In some cases, you may have to transfer the layout lines from one surface to another. It also helps to clearly mark the *waste side* of a layout line — the side on which you want to cut the kerf.

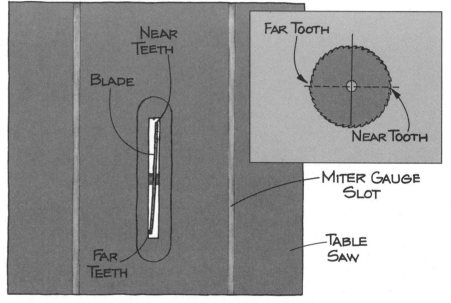

3-1 To accurately align the parts of a saw, you must compensate for "run-out" — the slight wobble that afflicts all saw blades. Using a rule, carefully measure the distance from the teeth on a saw blade to the miter gauge slot. As you rotate the saw blade, you'll find this distance isn't constant. Identify the "near" and the "far" teeth on the blade. Using a marker, draw a dotted line between these teeth, then a solid line perpendicular to the first. Both lines should pass through the center of the blade.

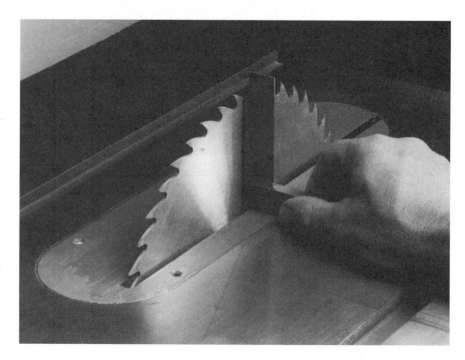

3-2 When checking the saw alignments, lay the square or triangle against the *solid* line on the blade. Or, measure from the teeth at either end of this line. These points will provide more accurate references than any others on the blade.

TRY THIS TRICK

When crosscutting on a table saw, it's sometimes difficult to position the board. Often, the surface with the layout line faces away from you, and to align this mark with the saw teeth, you must lean over the blade. A better method is to make and use a "third eye." Purchase an inspection mirror at an automotive store, cut off the handle, and mount the mirror on a small wooden base as shown. When you need to see something that faces away from you, place your third eye where it will reflect what you need to see.

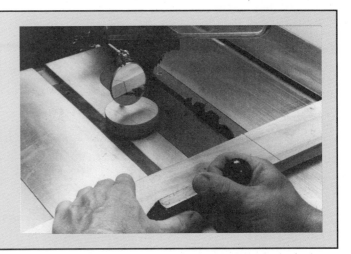

To make a cut, feed the wood into the blade slowly, using a steady, even pressure. Monitor the blade constantly, and slow down if it begins to bog down or vibrate. If the blade binds or burns in the cut, you could have a piece of reaction wood. Discard that board and get another. Vibration, bogging down, binding, and burning can also be caused by improper alignment. Check the tool setup carefully.

If you have to make duplicate cuts, feed each board at the same rate and with the same pressure. Remember that a saw, like any mechanical system, must have some "play." Although a miter gauge may seem snug in its slot, there has to be a little play or it won't move. As you push the gauge forward, put a little sideways pressure to the right or left to eliminate the play. Remember how hard and in which direction you pressed, then do the same on all remaining cuts.

This is an important technique! It ensures that duplicate cuts are *precise* duplicates, and it preserves the accuracy of your woodworking. Because there will always be a little play in your setups and you usually make more than one cut with each setup, you'll need to use this technique — or some variation of it — over and over again.

FOR BEST RESULTS

For joinery cuts, use a saw blade that leaves as smooth a surface as possible. You have several good choices. *Hollow-ground planer blades* (top) make an extremely smooth cut. However, they require more "projection" than other blades — the teeth must completely clear the work as you cut, or the blade will burn the wood. For this reason, they don't work well on radial arm saws. *Carbide-tipped combination blades* (bottom) with 40 teeth or more are smooth-cutting, require minimal projection, and can be used on both table saws and radial arm saws. Finally, *thin-kerf blades* (middle) also leave smooth cuts and are as versatile as carbide-tipped blades. They also cut faster with less friction; however, because the blades are so thin, thin-kerf blades are more prone to vibration. You may want to use large, specially made washers called blade stabilizers, available from most mail-order woodworking suppliers.

CUT-OFF JIG

Miter gauges offer little support when crosscutting large boards on a table saw. The face of the miter gauge is too small to keep the board properly aligned. You can attach an extension to the face of your miter gauge to gain extra support — some woodworkers fasten an extension between *two* miter gauges — but this is not a perfect solution, either. You must still contend with the friction of the wood as it slides across the worktable.

A cut-off jig solves both problems — it provides adequate support for large boards *and* relieves the friction. The sliding table of this particular cut-off jig is a large slab of medium-density fiberboard (MDF). (I used MDF because it remains very flat.) Two acrylic plastic runners ride in the miter gauge slots, guiding the jig's table back and forth across the table saw. A fence backs up the boards as you cut them.

This particular cut-off jig has several special fea-
tures. If you want to make duplicate cuts, the fence is grooved so you can mount a stop anywhere along its length. The grooved portion of the fence — the fence extension slide — can be extended to position the stop up to 36 inches away from the blade. If you want to hold the board down while you cut it, you can mount a clamp on the fence. (The straight-line toggle clamp shown is available from most mail-order woodworking suppliers.) And an acrylic plastic guard protects you from the saw blade.

The construction of the cut-off jig is straight-forward. Glue up stock to make the thick piece needed for the stop and the tieblock. Cut the sliding table from MDF; the stop, fence extension slide, fence top, middle, and bottom from solid hardwood; the runners and guard parts from acrylic plastic; and the remaining parts from plywood. **Note:** Make the fence extension slide and

1 **Before you can align the** fence or use the cut-off jig, cut a slot in the sliding table. Lower the blade beneath the table. Place the jig on the saw, fitting the runners in the miter gauge slots. The sliding table and the fence should straddle the saw blade. Turn the saw on, raise the blade, and push the jig forward, cutting a slot. The fence and the tieblock will keep the table together.

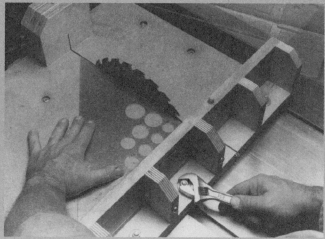

2 **Align the fence so it's** perpendicular to the blade in the same way you'd align a miter gauge. Raise the blade as high as possible and loosen the bolts that hold the fence to the sliding table. Use a drafting triangle to adjust the fence square to the blade, then tighten the bolts. **Note:** Make sure that the drafting triangle rests against the blade, but not the teeth.

fence middle in one long strip, then cut into two parts *after* routing the joinery.

Rout the grooves and rabbets in the fence parts, as shown in the *Fence Extension Slide Detail.* Cut the fence extension slide/fence middle into two parts, as shown in the *Top View.* Drill the bolt holes in the fence base a little larger than the bolts. This gives you the play necessary to align the fence precisely square to the blade.

Cut and drill five of the seven fence braces as shown in the *Fence Brace Layout,* and install threaded inserts and roundhead stove bolts in the holes. The fingers on these braces hold the fence extension slide in place. As you turn the bolts clockwise, they press the fingers forward and lock the extension in place. Turn them counterclockwise and the fingers spring back so you can easily move the extension. Assemble the fence with glue and flathead wood screws. Be careful *not* to glue the fence extension slide in place.

Cut and drill the stop as shown in the *Stop* drawings. Pay careful attention to the wood grain direction — it should be *parallel* to the stop's fingers. One face of the stop is pointed (as shown in the *Stop/Top View*) to keep sawdust from becoming trapped between the stop and the stock when making duplicate cuts.

Attach the tieblock to the sliding table with glue and flathead wood screws. Bolt the runners, fence assembly, and clamp assembly to the sliding table, but do *not* glue them in place.

Cut and drill the parts of the guard as shown in the *Guard* drawings. Note that one of the mounting holes is slightly larger than the other. This makes it possible to shift the fence slightly when you align it with the blade. Assemble the plastic parts with acrylic glue. Install a dowel in the fence and another in the tieblock to hold the guard in place.

3 **Use the cut-off jig as you** would a miter gauge. Rest a board against the fence, then slide the jig forward, past the blade. If you want to make duplicate cuts, secure the stop block to the fence by turning the wing nut. The block mounts in a groove in the fence.

4 **If you need to make** duplicate cuts longer than the fence, pull the fence extension slide sideways and lock it in place. The stop block groove in the middle portion enables you to mount the stop block out past the table.

(continued) ▷

CUT-OFF JIG — CONTINUED

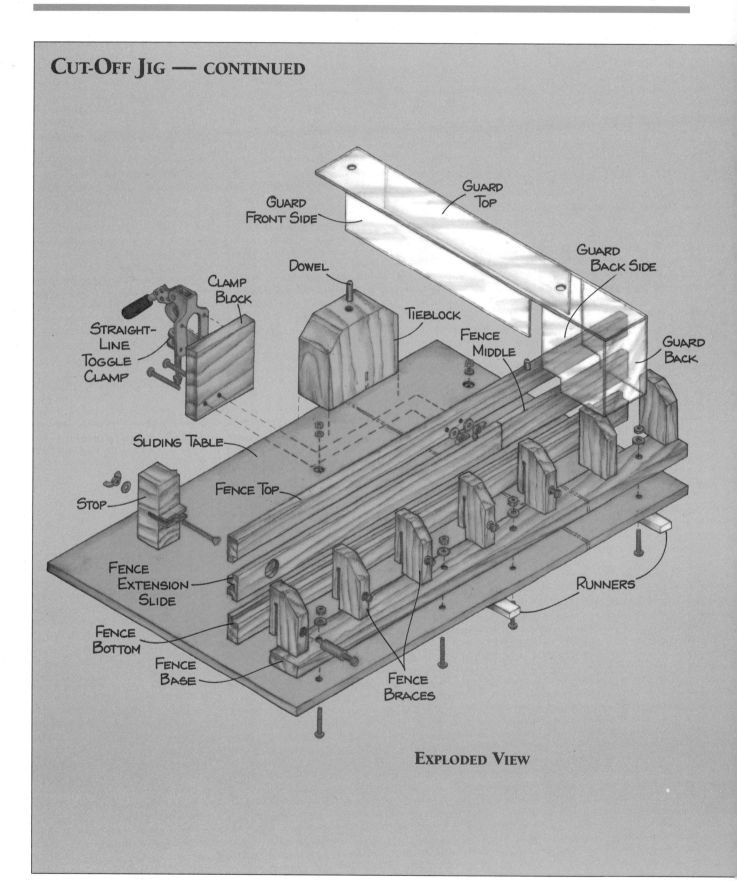

GUARD
FRONT SIDE

GUARD
TOP

GUARD
BACK SIDE

GUARD
BACK

DOWEL

TIEBLOCK

FENCE
MIDDLE

CLAMP
BLOCK

STRAIGHT-
LINE
TOGGLE
CLAMP

SLIDING TABLE

STOP

FENCE TOP

FENCE
EXTENSION
SLIDE

RUNNERS

FENCE
BOTTOM

FENCE
BASE

FENCE
BRACES

EXPLODED VIEW

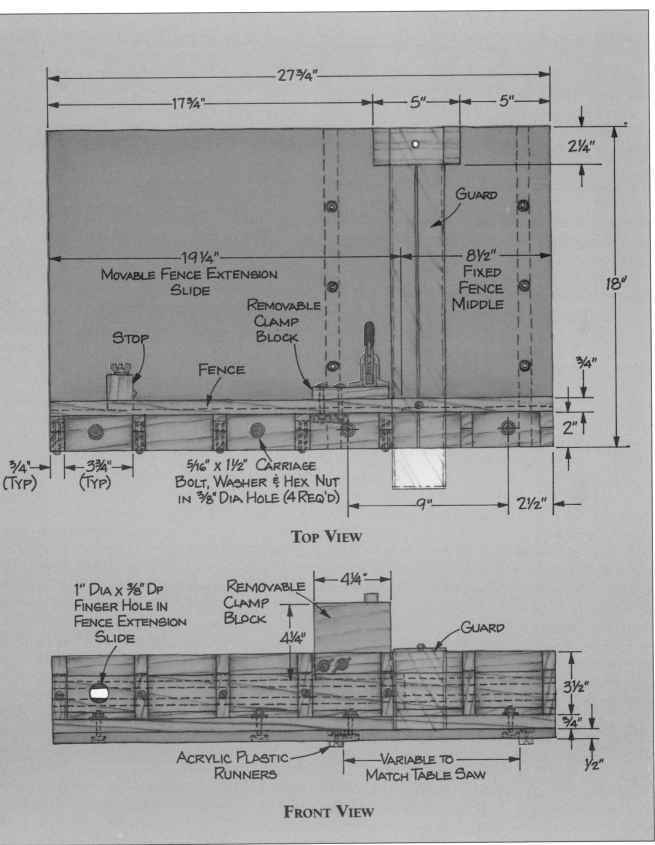

TOP VIEW

27¾"

17¾"

5"

5"

2¼"

GUARD

19¼"
MOVABLE FENCE EXTENSION
SLIDE

8½"
FIXED
FENCE
MIDDLE

18"

REMOVABLE
CLAMP
BLOCK

STOP

¾"

FENCE

2"

¾"
(TYP)

3¾"
(TYP)

5/16" x 1½" CARRIAGE
BOLT, WASHER & HEX NUT
IN ⅜" DIA HOLE (4 REQ'D)

9"

2½"

FRONT VIEW

1" DIA x ⅜" DP
FINGER HOLE IN
FENCE EXTENSION
SLIDE

REMOVABLE
CLAMP
BLOCK

4¼"

GUARD

4¼"

3½"

¾"

ACRYLIC PLASTIC
RUNNERS

VARIABLE TO
MATCH TABLE SAW

½"

(continued) ▷

CUT-OFF JIG — CONTINUED

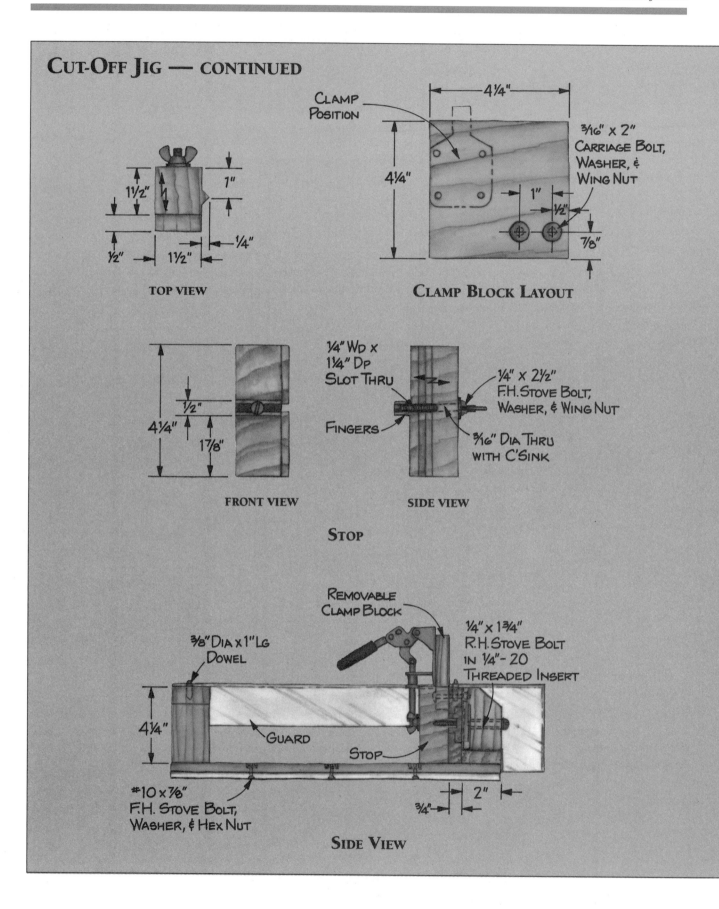

CLAMP POSITION

4¼"

4¼"

1"

1½"

¼"

½"   1½"

TOP VIEW

3⁄16" x 2" CARRIAGE BOLT, WASHER, & WING NUT

1"

½"

7⁄8"

CLAMP BLOCK LAYOUT

¼" WD x 1¼" DP SLOT THRU

4¼"

½"

1⁷⁄8"

FINGERS

¼" x 2½" F.H. STOVE BOLT, WASHER, & WING NUT

3⁄16" DIA THRU WITH C'SINK

FRONT VIEW   **SIDE VIEW**

STOP

REMOVABLE CLAMP BLOCK

3⁄8" DIA x 1" LG DOWEL

¼" x 1¾" R.H. STOVE BOLT IN ¼"- 20 THREADED INSERT

4¼"

GUARD

STOP

2"

¾"

#10 x ⁷⁄8" F.H. STOVE BOLT, WASHER, & HEX NUT

SIDE VIEW

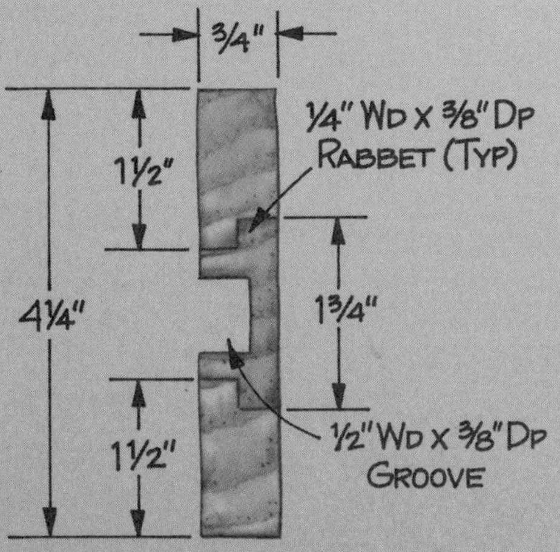
3/4"
1/4" Wd x 3/8" Dp
Rabbet (Typ)
1 1/2"
4 1/4"
1 3/4"
1 1/2"
1/2" Wd x 3/8" Dp
Groove

END VIEW

Fence Extension Slide Detail

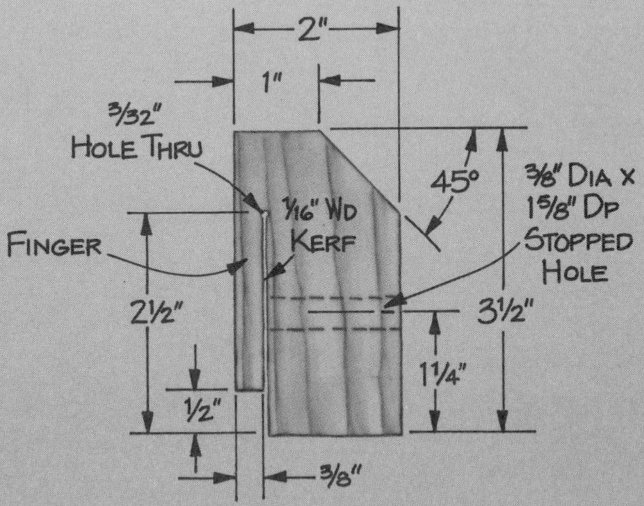
2"
1"
3/32"
Hole Thru
45°
3/8" Dia x
1 5/8" Dp
Stopped
Hole
1/16" Wd
Kerf
Finger
2 1/2"
3 1/2"
1 1/4"
1/2"
3/8"

Fence Brace Layout

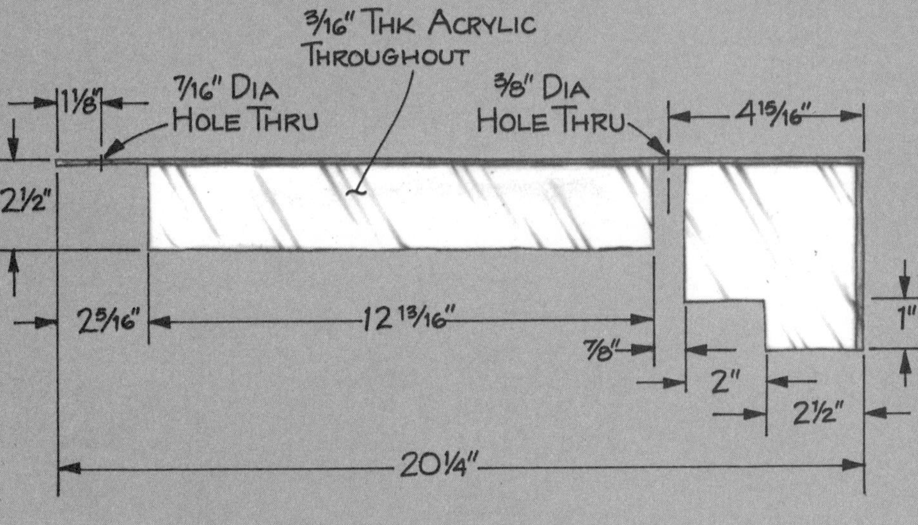
3/16" Thk Acrylic
Throughout
1 1/8"
7/16" Dia
Hole Thru
3/8" Dia
Hole Thru
4 15/16"
2 1/2"
2 5/16"
12 13/16"
7/8"
1"
2"
2 1/2"
20 1/4"

SIDE VIEW

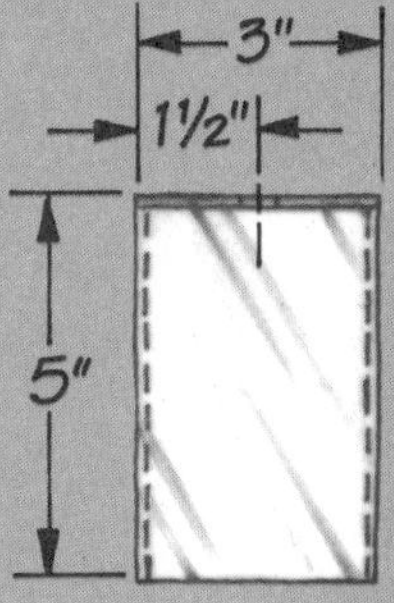
3"
1 1/2"
5"

END VIEW

Guard

MAKING MITER CUTS

There is little difference between making a butt cut and making a miter cut. If you're making the cut on a table saw, set the miter gauge to the proper angle. If you're using a radial arm saw, set the arm. To make a cut of 30, 45, or 60 degrees, use a drafting triangle to set the miter gauge or the arm. To make a cut at some other angle, use a protractor and a sliding T-bevel.

The procedure is similar if you're cutting a bevel, but you must set the blade at the proper angle. Measure the angle between the blade and the table with a triangle or protractor — the degree markings on the saw are notoriously inaccurate.

Always cut a few test pieces with this setup *before* you cut good stock. Make at least two miter cuts, hold the parts together, and measure the angle between them. (*See Figure 3-3.*) Some woodworkers prefer to make a miniature frame from test stock. Cut the required number of frame members to precisely the same length and miter the ends. Fit the pieces together. If there are no gaps in any of the miters, then the setup is adjusted to the proper angle.

In addition to cutting simple miters and bevels, you can also make *compound miters,* mitering *and* beveling a board at the same time. Compound miters are used to assemble moldings and sloping frames, in which the faces of the frame members rest at angles instead of presenting a flat face or edge. The angle or *slope* of the frame members determines the miter and bevel angles. Consult "Compound Miter Angles" on the facing page for the proper settings for both the miter gauge (or saw arm) and the saw blade. (*See Figures 3-4 and 3-5.*)

3-3 **To test a miter setup, cut two** test pieces and hold the mitered ends together. Measure the angle between the pieces with a square or sliding T-bevel. If the angle is *smaller* than you hoped for and the square or protractor won't fit between the test pieces, *increase* the angle of the miter gauge. If the angle is *larger,* and there's a gap between the test pieces and the measuring device, then *decrease* the miter gauge angle.

3-4 **To cut a compound miter, set** the miter gauge at an angle *and* tilt the saw blade. The gauge angle and the blade angle are determined by both the number of sides in the frame you want to make and the *slope* of its members.

3-5 To check the setup, cut a test frame and assemble the members with masking tape. Measure the slope with a sliding T-bevel and a protractor. If the slope is *steeper* than you want, *decrease* the angle of the miter gauge. If it's *shallower, increase* the angle. Also inspect the joints. If they open on the *outside, increase* the tilt of the blade. If they open on the *inside, decrease* the tilt. Make these adjustments slowly, changing the miter gauge angle and the blade tilt no more than ½ degree at a time. You may have to cut several test frames before the setup is adjusted properly.

COMPOUND MITER ANGLES

FOUR SIDES			SIX SIDES		
SLOPE* OF FRAME	MITER GAUGE OR SAW ARM ANGLE†	SAW BLADE ANGLE	SLOPE* OF FRAME	MITER GAUGE OR SAW ARM ANGLE†	SAW BLADE ANGLE
85°	86°	44¾°	85°	87½°	29¾°
80°	82¼°	44¼°	80°	84¾°	29½°
75°	78¼°	43½°	75°	82¼°	29°
70°	74½°	42¼°	70°	79¾°	28¼°
65°	71°	40¾°	65°	77¼°	27¼°
60°	67½°	39°	60°	75°	26°
55°	64¼°	36¾°	55°	72¾°	24½°
50°	61°	34½°	50°	70¾°	23°
45°	58¼°	31¾°	45°	68¾°	21¼°
40°	55½°	29°	40°	67°	19¼°
35°	53¼°	25¾°	35°	65½°	17¼°
30°	51°	22½°	30°	64°	15°
25°	49¼°	19°	25°	62¾°	12¾°
20°	47¾°	15½°	20°	61¾°	10¼°
15°	46½°	11¾°	15°	61°	7¾°
10°	45¾°	7¾°	10°	60½°	5¼°
5°	45¼°	4°	5°	60°	2½°

EIGHT SIDES					
85°	88°	22½°	35°	71½°	13°
80°	86°	22¼°	30°	70½°	11¼°
75°	84¼°	21¾°	25°	69½°	9½°
70°	82¼°	21¼°	20°	68¾°	7¾°
65°	80½°	20½°	15°	68¼°	5¾°
60°	78¾°	19½°	10°	67¾°	4°
55°	77°	18½°	5°	67½°	2°
50°	75½°	17¼°			
45°	74°	16°	*The slope of the stock's face, as measured from horizontal.		
40°	72¾°	14½°	† For the proper saw arm setting, subtract the angle shown on the chart from 90°.		

MITER JIG

If you make many miter cuts, you may tire of constantly readjusting your miter gauge to the proper angle. Instead, you can set this jig to any angle between 70 and 30 degrees (approximately), then *leave it* so it's always ready to go. And if you regularly cut several miter angles, build several jigs and set each to the appropriate angle.

The sliding table is made of medium-density fiberboard (MDF), with two acrylic plastic runners that ride in the miter gauge slots, guiding the jig's table back and forth across the table saw. Two adjustable fences, one for making left-facing miters and the other for right-facing miters, back up the stock as you cut it.

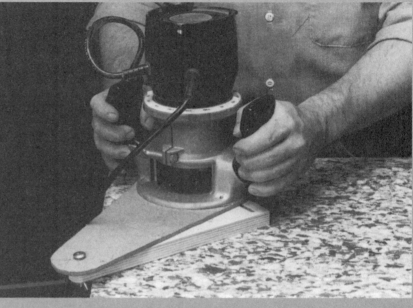

1 **Rout the curved slots in the** adjustable fences with a router and a *Circle-Cutting Jig.* This simple jig is a piece of ¼-inch plywood cut to fit the base of your router. Drill a ¼-inch-diameter pivot hole in the plywood, 9¼ inches from the router bit. Rout the slot in several passes, cutting ⅛ inch to ¼ inch deeper with each pass.

2 **Place the jig on the table** saw so the runners fit in the miter gauge slots, and cut a saw kerf in the sliding table. Do *not* cut all the way through the table. Stop the kerf just past the fences. Turn off the saw and use a drafting triangle, square, protractor, or sliding T-bevel to adjust the fences. Afterwards, make several test cuts with each fence to ensure it is set properly.

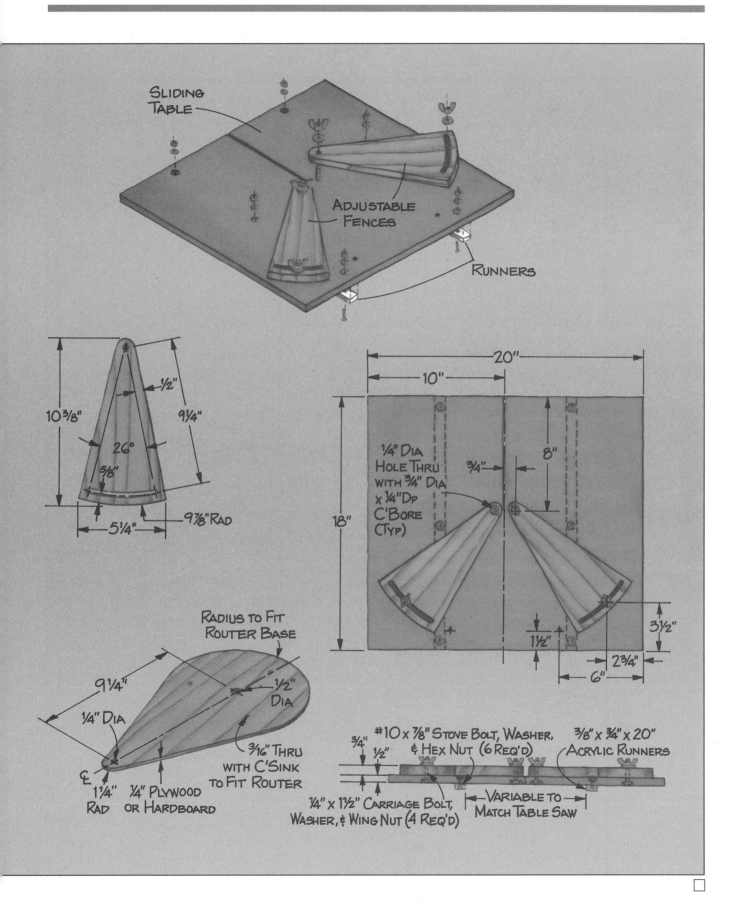

SLIDING TABLE

ADJUSTABLE FENCES

RUNNERS

10³⁄₈"
½"
9¼"
26°
5⁄₈"
5¼"
9⅞" RAD

20"
10"
¼" DIA HOLE THRU WITH ¾" DIA x ¼" DP C'BORE (TYP)
¾"
8"
18"
3½"
1½"
2¾"
6"

RADIUS TO FIT ROUTER BASE
9¼"
½" DIA
¼" DIA
3⁄16" THRU WITH C'SINK TO FIT ROUTER
1¼" RAD
¼" PLYWOOD OR HARDBOARD
₵

¾"
½"
#10 x ⅞" STOVE BOLT, WASHER, & HEX NUT (6 REQ'D)
3⁄8" x ¾" x 20" ACRYLIC RUNNERS
¼" x 1½" CARRIAGE BOLT, WASHER, & WING NUT (4 REQ'D)
VARIABLE TO MATCH TABLE SAW

MAKING RABBET CUTS

You can make a rabbet with either a table-mounted router and a straight bit, or a table saw and a dado cutter. For either setup, use a fence to guide the work. Adjust the width of the rabbet by changing the position of the fence relative to the bit or cutter. Adjust the depth by changing the height of the bit or cutter above the table.

Cut a rabbet in a test piece, feeding the wood past the bit or cutter. (Remember to feed the wood *against* the rotation of the cutting tool.) Measure the width and depth of the rabbet and, if necessary, adjust the position of the fence or the height of the cutter. Then cut the good stock. (*SEE FIGURES 3-6 AND 3-7.*)

You can also use a table saw and an ordinary saw blade to cut a rabbet, but this requires two passes and — almost always — two setups. Cut the larger dimension first, then the smaller. Since you must perform this operation without the saw guard, this sequence will leave less blade exposed when the waste stock falls away from the workpiece. (*SEE FIGURE 3-8.*)

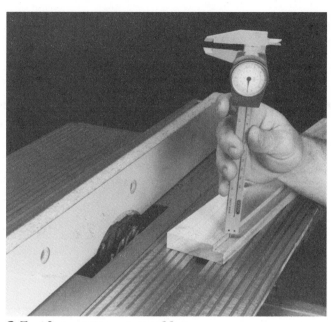

3-7 After cutting a test rabbet, measure the width and the depth. You can use a small rule for this, or — if you want to be more precise — use the depth gauge on your calipers.

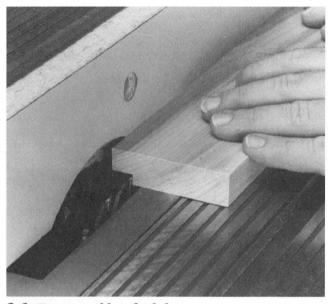

3-6 To cut a rabbet, feed the board past the bit or cutter, keeping it pressed against both the table and the fence. Note that the fence is faced with a board, and this board has a cutout the same diameter as the cutter. The board protects both the fence *and* you. It keeps the cutter from biting into the metal fence, and the cutout surrounds the unused portion of the cutter. *Never* cut a rabbet with part of the bit or cutter exposed.

3-8 When cutting a rabbet with an ordinary saw blade, you must make two passes. On the second pass, position the workpiece so the waste will be on the side of the blade farthest from the fence. If you make the cut with the waste between the fence and the blade, the waste will kick back.

After cutting a rabbet with a dado cutter or a saw blade, inspect the inside corner between the side and the bottom. These cutting tools sometimes leave a little waste or "tang" in the corner. You can quickly remove this with a scraper, chisel, or bullnose plane.

MAKING DADO CUTS

Like a rabbet, a dado can be made with either a table-mounted router and a straight bit, or a table saw and a dado cutter. The adjustments, however, are not quite the same. Adjust the width of the dado by changing the width of the cutter or the diameter of the bit; adjust the depth by raising or lowering the bit or cutter. Finally, position the dado by changing the position of the workpiece relative to the cutter.

There are several ways to guide the workpiece. If you're making a groove (cutting *with* the wood grain), use a fence to guide the workpiece over the bit or cutter. If you're making a dado (cutting *across* the grain), use a miter gauge. If the workpiece is too large to guide easily with a miter gauge, clamp a straightedge to the workpiece and use it to guide a portable router. (*SEE FIGURE 3-9.*)

3-9 Use a portable router to make a dado or a rabbet if the board is too large to cut on a table saw or a table-mounted router. Clamp a straight-edge to the workpiece to guide the router. Here, a shopmade T-square automatically aligns the straightedge at 90 degrees to the edge of the board.

In a pinch, you can cut a dado with an ordinary saw blade and some hand tools. Saw the sides of the dado to the proper depth and remove most of the waste with a chisel. Then clean up the bottom of the dado with a router plane.

MAKING MORTISES

There are many different ways to make a mortise, but we'll concentrate on three of the easiest. Perhaps the simplest of all is to use a drill press. Lay out the mortise, remove as much waste as possible by drilling overlapping holes, then clean up the sides and corners with a chisel. (SEE FIGURES 5-2 THROUGH 5-4.) If you have less than a dozen mortises to make, this is an excellent method. And because there is little setup time, it's very quick.

5-2 To make a mortise on a drill press, first lay out the joint on the stock with a marking gauge and an awl. In addition to marking the perimeter of the mortise, scribe a line down the center to help position the drill bit.

5-3 Select a bit diameter that matches the width of the mortise you want to make. (Some woodworkers prefer to use a bit that is *slightly* smaller.) Mount the bit in the drill press and bore overlapping holes to remove most of the waste from the mortise. Don't space the holes too close; the bit may drift. If you wish, clamp a straightedge to the drill press to guide the stock. This will keep the holes in a perfectly straight line.

5-4 Remove the remaining waste from the sides and ends of the mortise with chisels. Use an ordinary beveled-edge paring chisel to clean up the sides and — if you have one — a mortising chisel to square the ends.

FOR BEST RESULTS

When cleaning up a mortise, use a *mortising chisel* to square the ends or remove large amounts of stock. Most chisels are designed to be used alternately as a cutting tool and a wedge — you cut down through the grain, then split out the waste. A mortise leaves little room to work in this manner, so a mortising chisel splits *as* it cuts. The thick blade with its steep bevel pushes the waste to one side as you cut down through the wood. **Note:** Always place the cutting edge of a mortising chisel *across* the wood grain.

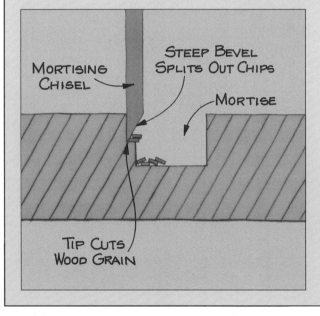

You can also use a hand-held or table-mounted router and a straight bit to cut a mortise. Simply rout a double-blind dado in the stock, then square the blind ends with a chisel. (*SEE FIGURES 5-5 THROUGH 5-10.*) This method requires more setup time, but saves cutting time, particularly if you have a lot of mortises to make. The drawback is that you can only make relatively shallow mortises, no deeper than the router bit will reach.

When routing a mortise, make the recess in several passes. Remove just $1/8$ to $1/4$ inch of stock with each pass — remember that routers and router bits aren't designed to remove large amounts of stock all at once. If you have a lot of mortises to rout, adjust the router to cut no more than $1/4$ inch deep. Cut all the mortises in all the workpieces to this depth. Increase the depth of cut and rout all the mortises again. Continue until you have routed the mortises as deep as you want them.

5-5 To rout a mortise with a hand-held router, make a frame to guide the router. Clamp the frame to the workpiece and rout the mortise, keeping the base of the router inside the frame. The inside dimensions of the frame will control the length and width of the mortise. **Note:** If you have one, use a plunge router when performing this operation. Otherwise, you may want to drill a stopped hole that's a little larger than the router bit into the middle of the mortise. This will provide a place to start routing.

TRY THIS TRICK

If you wish, use a mortising fence to make multiple mortises. This jig has adjustable stops at both ends to automatically start and stop mortise cuts, and can be used on both a drill press and a router table. Plans and instructions for making this "Mortising Fence" are on page 67.

5-6 You can also use a guide collar and a template to make a mortise with a hand-held router. Mount the guide collar on the router sole with the bit protruding through the center. Clamp the template to the workpiece and rout the mortise, following the inside edges of the template with the collar. This setup is especially useful for routing small mortises.

5-7 When routing a mortise on a table-mounted router, it's difficult to know where to start and stop since you can't see the cut as it progresses. To remedy this situation, make several alignment marks where they will be visible on both the machine and the workpiece. First, put a piece of tape on the fence or on the work surface of the router table. Using a small square, mark the diameter of the bit on the tape.

5-8 Next, use the square to transfer the layout lines that mark the *length* of the mortise to another surface on the workpiece. This surface must be clearly visible when you cut.

5-9 Select a router bit that's the same diameter as the width of the mortise you want to make. Mount it in the router and adjust the depth of cut to cut no more than ⅛–¼ inch at one time. Secure a fence or straightedge to the router table to guide the workpiece. Hold the workpiece firmly against the fence with the area to be mortised above the bit. (If possible, let one end of the workpiece rest on an edge of the table.) Turn the router on and carefully lower the workpiece onto the bit.

5-10 Feed the work to the right until the left-hand mark on the workpiece lines up with the left-hand mark on the router table. Then feed it back to the left until the right-hand marks line up. As you're cutting, keep the stock firmly against the fence or straightedge. Finally, turn off the router and let it come to a complete stop before removing the workpiece. **Note:** A foot-operated switch is very handy for this operation.

Finally, you can use a mortiser or a mortising attachment to make a mortise. As mentioned previously, a mortiser makes a *square* hole. Drill a series of overlapping square holes to form the rectangular mortise. (*SEE FIGURES 5-11 AND 5-12.*) Of the three methods, this requires the most setup time, particularly if you have to mount the mortising attachment on a drill press.

But it eliminates all hand work; you don't have to clean up the mortises with a chisel. If you make a lot of mortises, this will save time. The drawback is that a mortiser is a finicky tool that must be set up and operated with special care. Refer to "Using a Mortiser" on page 69 for more information.

5-11 Use a mortising attachment on a drill press to bore a row of overlapping *square* holes, in much the same way you would bore overlapping round holes. These holes will form a mortise without your having to clean up the sides or square the ends.

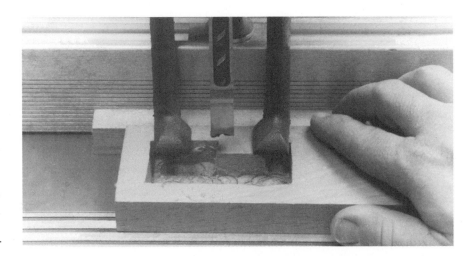

5-12 If the mortise you want to make is wider than the chisels that are available for the mortising accessory, drill two or more rows of overlapping square holes. Overlap the rows as well as the holes in the rows.

MORTISING FENCE

This specialized fence helps to automatically size mortises. It guides the work past a bit or cutter *and* stops the cut when the mortise is the proper length. The fence accommodates both long and short workpieces, and can be clamped or bolted to either a drill press or a router table.

Make the fence face, base, and braces from cabinet-grade plywood. Cut a slot in the face, then assemble the parts with glue and screws. Make the stops from hardwood and drill them for dowels and carriage bolts. Note that the *inside* edges of the stops are mitered. This prevents sawdust from accumulating between the stops and the workpiece, where it would interfere with the accuracy of the cut.

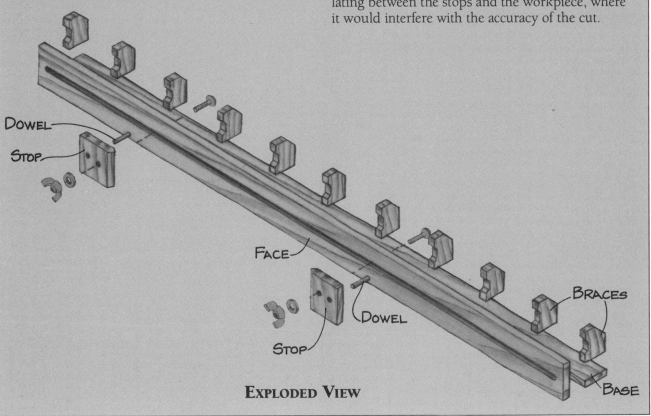

DOWEL

STOP

FACE

STOP

DOWEL

BRACES

BASE

EXPLODED VIEW

(continued) ▷

MORTISING FENCE — CONTINUED

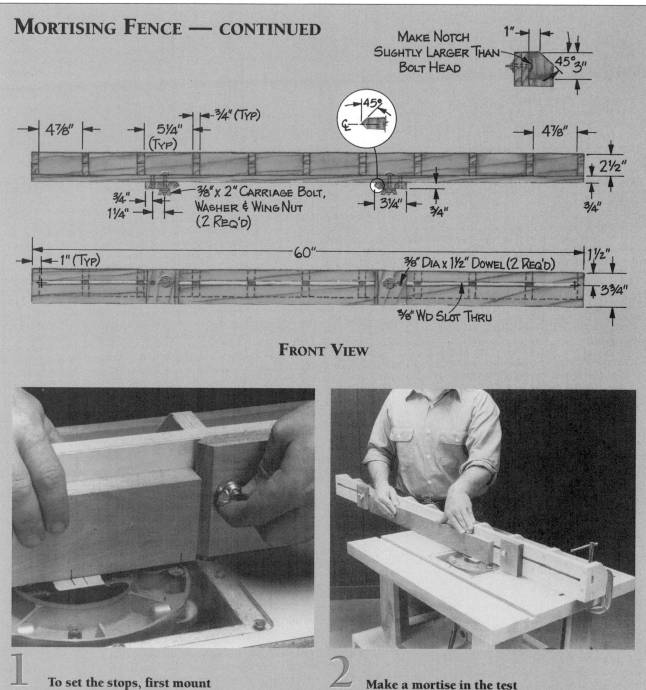

MAKE NOTCH
SLIGHTLY LARGER THAN
BOLT HEAD

FRONT VIEW

1 **To set the stops, first mount** the fence on a drill press or router table. Carefully lay out a mortise on a test piece. Place the test piece on the worktable and position it as if you were about to begin cutting. Set the stop on the appropriate end of the fence. Next, move the piece to where you want to stop cutting and set the other stop.

2 **Make a mortise in the test** piece, using the stops to control the length of the cut. If the completed mortise matches the layout lines, the stops are set accurately. If not, adjust the position of the stops as needed. When the stops are set where you want them, cut the good stock.

USING A MORTISER

A mortiser drills a square hole by combining the action of a chisel and a drill bit. A square, hollow chisel attaches to the drill press quill and moves up and down. A bit mounts in the chuck and spins inside the chisel. As you feed both cutting tools into the wood, the bit drills a round hole and the chisel trims it square. The edges of the chisel are beveled to direct the chips into the bit, which carries them up and out of the way.

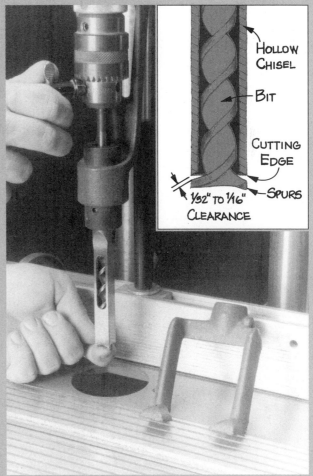

1 **In setting up a mortiser,** employ a fence to guide the workpiece. Use a small square to position the chisel so the front and back surfaces are parallel to the fence. If they aren't, the sides of the mortise won't be straight. Adjust the mortiser's hold-down to keep the stock flat on the table. Otherwise, you'll find it difficult to retract the bit.

2 **Adjust the clearance between** the spurs on the bit and the end of the chisel to no less than $1/32$ inch and no more than $1/16$ inch. **This is very important!** If the clearance is too little, the bit will rub on the chisel. The resulting friction will heat the chisel and the bit, ruining both. If it's too large, the spurs won't break up the wood chips, and they will clog the chisel.

(continued) ▷

Using a Mortiser — continued

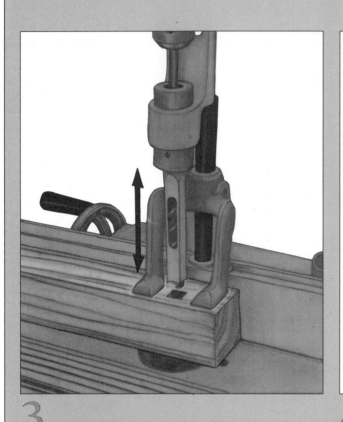

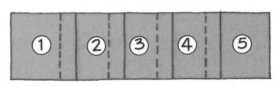

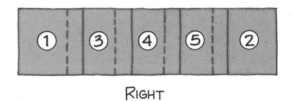

3 **When drilling a square hole,** feed the chisel slowly with a firm pressure. Give the tool plenty of time to clear the chips. It also helps to retract the chisel often. Plunge the chisel into the wood, hold the pressure for a few seconds, retract the chisel, and repeat. (This technique is especially useful when mortising hardwoods.) If you have to use excessive pressure to drill a hole, there is something wrong with your setup — most probably, the clearance between the bit and the chisel is incorrect or the cutting tools are dull.

4 **When drilling a row of over-**lapping square holes, you must make the cuts in the proper sequence. Drill the ends of the mortise first, then go back and remove the waste between them. Ideally, the overlapping portion of the holes should be no more than one-quarter the width of the chisel — otherwise, the chisel may drift in the cut.

MAKING AND FITTING TENONS

There are also many ways to make a tenon. Again, here are three of the easiest.

Many woodworkers prefer to make tenons on a table saw with an ordinary blade. First, cut the shoulders of the tenon, using a miter gauge to guide the workpiece. Then cut the cheeks, using a tenoning jig. (For instructions and plans on how to make this fixture, see the "Tenoning Jig" on page 72.) Test fit the tenon to its mortise and adjust the setup as needed. *(SEE FIGURES 5-13 AND 5-14.)*

5-13 To cut a tenon with an ordinary table saw blade, first cut the shoulders. Guide the stock with a miter gauge. If you wish, use the fence to position the stock on the gauge.

5-14 Next, cut the cheeks, using a tenoning jig to hold the stock as you slide the jig along the fence. Test fit the tenon in its mortise. If it's too *tight,* move the fence *closer* to the blade — this will shave a little more stock from the tenon. If it's too *loose,* move the fence *farther away* — this will make the tenon thicker.

You can also make a tenon with a dado cutter. The advantage to using this accessory is that you can cut both a shoulder and a cheek in one pass. You also have a choice of using either the tenoning jig or the miter gauge to guide the stock. (*See Figures 5-15 and 5-16.*) The disadvantage is that it usually requires more setup time — you have to remove the blade from your table saw and mount the dado cutter.

5-15 To cut a tenon with a dado cutter, mount the workpiece in a tenoning jig. Back up the workpiece with a scrap board to prevent the cutter from tearing the wood grain when it exits the workpiece. Then guide the jig along the fence, past the cutter.

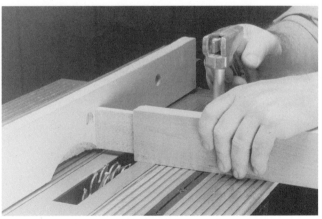

5-16 You can also use a miter gauge to guide the workpiece when cutting a tenon with a dado cutter. This setup allows you to make much longer tenons, since you aren't limited by the diameter of the cutter. It's also easier to cut shoulders and cheeks on all four sides of a tenon. The disadvantage is that you usually must make several passes to cut each tenon side.

Finally, you can cut a tenon on a table-mounted router, using a miter gauge to guide the workpiece over a straight bit. *(SEE FIGURE 5-17.)* Like a routed mortise, a routed tenon requires multiple passes over the bit — if you have lots of tenons to make, this isn't the tool to use. However, the routed cheeks and shoulders are extremely smooth. If the fit of the tenon or the strength of the glue bond is paramount, use a router.

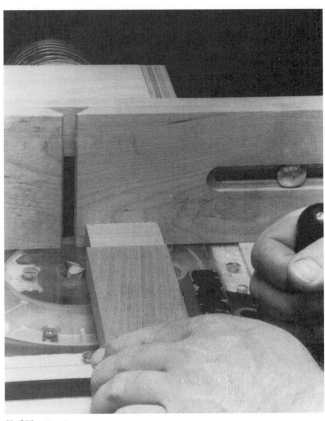

5-17 You can cut a tenon on a table-mounted router using a miter gauge to guide the tenon over the bit. Prevent the workpiece from creeping across the face of the gauge by positioning the fence just behind the bit. Make sure this fence is precisely parallel to the miter gauge slot, or the cut won't be accurate.

TRY THIS TRICK

To fit a mortise-and-tenon joint with no gap between the adjoining parts, it may help to undercut the shoulders of the tenon. Using a chisel, remove a small amount of stock from the shoulder where it meets the cheek.

UNDERCUT SHOULDER

TENONING JIG

A tenoning jig holds a workpiece vertically to make a cut in its end. This particular jig rides along the table saw fence, like the "Splined Miter Jig" on page 56. The workpiece rests against a quadrant, and a clamp secures the workpiece to the vertical face of the jig. You can adjust the angle of the workpiece between 45 and 90 degrees by rotating the quadrant.

Make the vertical face and the spacer from ³/₄-inch cabinet-grade plywood, and the remaining parts from hardwood. Cut or rout the slots in the spacer and the quadrant. Also make the dado in the vertical face. Drill the holes needed to mount the quadrant and the clamp.

Glue and screw the spacer to the face. Secure the quadrant to the face with carriage bolts, washers, and wing nuts. (Note that there are six mounting holes, and the quadrant can be attached in four different positions.) Attach the leg to the spacer with roundhead wood screws and washers. Adjust the gap between the leg and the face to fit your table saw fence, then tighten the wing nuts.

(continued) ▷

TENONING JIG — CONTINUED

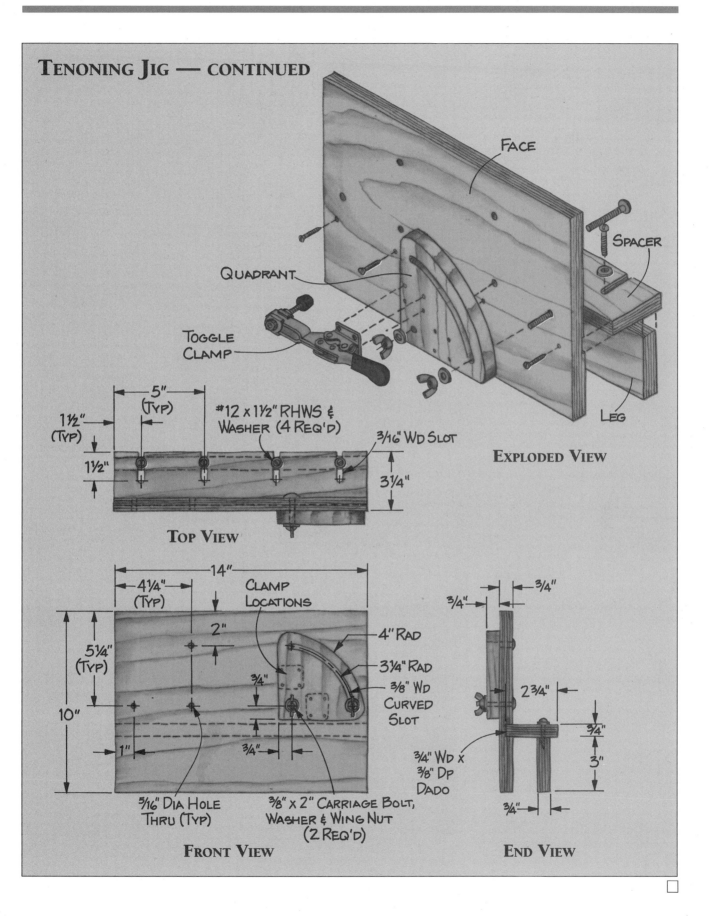

FACE

SPACER

QUADRANT

TOGGLE CLAMP

LEG

EXPLODED VIEW

5" (TYP)

1½" (TYP)

1½"

#12 x 1½" RHWS & WASHER (4 REQ'D)

3/16" WD SLOT

3¼"

TOP VIEW

14"

4¼" (TYP)

CLAMP LOCATIONS

2"

4" RAD

3¼" RAD

5¼" (TYP)

¾"

3/8" WD CURVED SLOT

10"

1"

¾"

5/16" DIA HOLE THRU (TYP)

3/8" x 2" CARRIAGE BOLT, WASHER & WING NUT (2 REQ'D)

FRONT VIEW

¾"

¾"

¾"

2¾"

¾"

3"

¾"

3/4" WD X 3/8" DP DADO

END VIEW

VARIATIONS

Here are three useful variations on the mortise and tenon:

Slot mortise and tenon — This is more commonly called a bridle joint. Both the mortise and the tenon are "open" — that is, visible from the ends of the adjoining boards. This greatly simplifies the mortising operation. In fact, you can cut both the mortise and the tenon with a single setup. (*SEE FIGURES 5-18 THROUGH 5-20.*) **Note:** As shown in the photos, this operation will make bridle joints in ³/₄-inch-thick stock. To use other thicknesses, change the thickness and/or number of spacers. You can also use a dado cutter instead of a saw blade.

5-18 You can make a bridle joint in ³/₄-inch-thick stock with one simple table saw setup. Clamp two ¹/₈-inch-thick spacers to the fence. Adjust the "Tenoning Jig" shown on page 72 to span the spacers, and position the fence to hold the jig ³/₈ inch away from the saw blade. Mount one of the members in the jig. To keep the blade from tearing the stock when it exits the cut, back up the stock with a scrap. Cut the mortise in two passes — run the stock over the blade, turn it edge for edge, and repeat. This will make a ¹/₄-inch-wide slot mortise.

5-19 The tenon requires *four* passes. To make the first two, remove *one* of the spacers from the blade side of the fence and attach it to the opposite side. Mount the second adjoining member in the jig and cut the tenon. Pass the stock over the blade, turn it edge for edge, and repeat.

5-20 Remove the last spacer from the blade side of the fence and transfer it to the opposite side. *Both* spacers should be clamped to the side of the fence facing away from the blade. Make another pass, turn the board, and repeat. This will complete the tenon.

Haunched mortise and tenon — This joint is useful for assembling paneled doors and other frame-and-panel constructions. In making this joint, you cut grooves along the entire length of both the rails and the stiles. When you assemble the rails and stiles, the grooves will hold a panel. The "haunch" on each tenon will fill the groove where it cuts across the mortise. (*SEE FIGURES 5-21 THROUGH 5-24.*)

5-21   To make a haunched mortise-and-tenon joint, first cut or rout grooves in the *inside* edges of the adjoining rails and stiles. These grooves most be centered in the edges of the stock. Later, when the rails and stiles are assembled, the grooves will hold a panel.

5-22   Rout or drill mortises in the stiles and square the ends. These mortises must be precisely the same width as the grooves. The *outside* ends of the mortises (closest to the ends of the boards) should be at least $1/4$ inch from the ends of the stiles. The distance from the ends of the stiles to the *inside* ends of the mortises (closest to the middle of the boards) should match the width of the rails less the depth of the groove.

5-23   Rout or cut tenons to fit the mortises. The tenons must be as thick as the grooves are wide. Each tenon should be as long as its mortise is deep (including the depth of the groove), minus $1/16$ inch. This small space will leave room for glue.

5-24 Cut or rout a corner notch in the outside edge of each tenon to create the haunch. The width of this notch must match the distance from the end of the stile to the outside end of the mortise. The distance from the shoulder of the tenon to the end of the haunch must match the depth of the groove. When the joint is assembled, the haunch of the tenon will fill the groove.

Round mortise-and-tenon — This joint is used to assemble turned parts, such as chair legs and rungs. Unlike other mortise-and-tenon joints, it must be cut with a drill and/or a lathe. *(SEE FIGURES 5-25 THROUGH 5-29.)* This is not a difficult joint to make, but requires special procedures. Here are a few things to consider when making it:

■ The *proportions* of the mortise and tenon are very important to the strength of the joint. The mortise should be at least 1½ times as deep as it is in diameter. The same holds true for the length of the tenon.

■ The surface of the mortise must be cut as cleanly as possible. Use a very sharp bit to drill the hole, and feed it slowly.

■ Use a V-jig to keep the turning from rolling when you drill the mortise.

■ If you drill the mortise all the way through the stock, the drill may tear out the wood grain as it exits the piece. To prevent this, drill a hole the same diameter as your stock through a thick scrap. Cut the scrap, splitting the hole in half. Use the scrap pieces, rather than the V-jig, to support the work.

TRY THIS TRICK

When making round mortises, you often have to drill two or more in a straight line along the length of a turning. To mark a straight line on round stock, hold the stock in the V created by a door jamb and its door stop. Using the stop as a straightedge, scribe a line down the length of the turning.

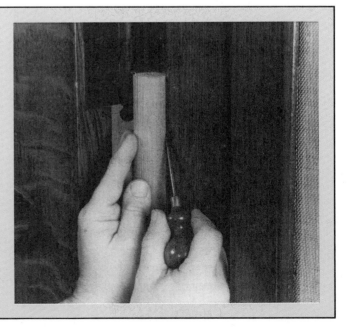

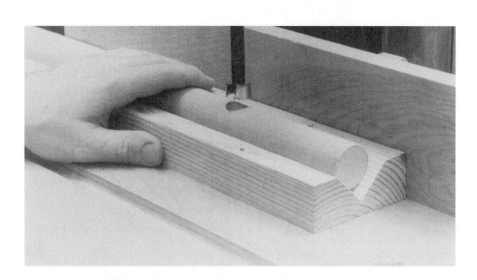

5-25 To drill a stopped round mortise in round stock, cradle the wood in a V-jig. Position the jig so the point of the bit is directly above the point of the V.

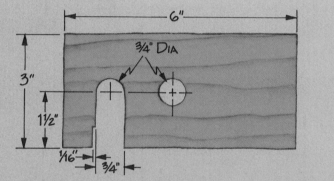

SAMPLE LAYOUT FOR FIXED CALIPERS
(FOR TURNING ¾" DIA TENONS)

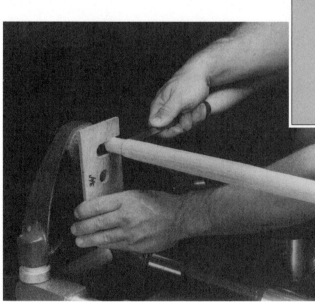

5-26 Turn the tenon to fit the mortise, using calipers to gauge the diameter of the tenon. You can make "fixed" calipers, as shown, from a scrap of ¼-inch plywood. This particular caliper has a ¹⁄₁₆-inch step cut in the opening to warn you when the tenon is approaching the finished diameter. Turn the stock until *just the step* in the caliper fits over the tenon.

5-27 Next, turn the tenon with *very* light cuts until the caliper fits completely over the tenon. Some woodworkers prefer to sand a tenon to its final diameter. Sandpaper removes stock more slowly than a chisel, reducing the chance that you might make the tenon too small.

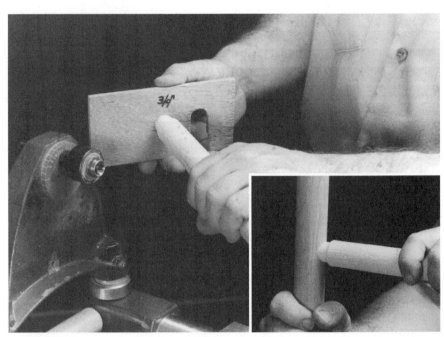

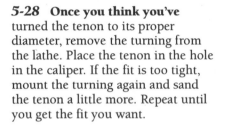

5-28 Once you think you've turned the tenon to its proper diameter, remove the turning from the lathe. Place the tenon in the hole in the caliper. If the fit is too tight, mount the turning again and sand the tenon a little more. Repeat until you get the fit you want.

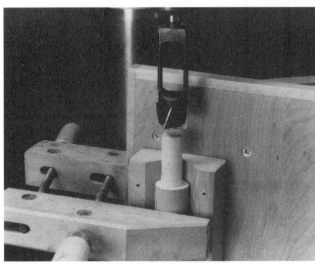

5-29 You can cut perfectly sized tenons on a drill press with a tenon cutter. (These specialized bits are available from most mail-order wood-working suppliers.) To use this accessory, first turn the tenon ⅛ to ¼ inch larger in diameter than needed. Mount the cutter in the drill press chuck and rotate the table to hold the turning *vertically*. Place the turning in a V-jig and clamp both the turning and the jig to the table, directly beneath the cutter. Turn on the drill press and slowly advance the quill, cutting the tenon to the proper diameter and length.

5-30 You can also use a tenon cutter to create round tenons on the ends of square or rectangular boards. Cut the tenons to the proper length on a drill press, then cut away any waste stock left by the cutter with a band saw or coping saw.

PEGGING A MORTISE-AND-TENON JOINT

Craftsmen sometimes secure a tenon in a mortise by driving one or more pegs through the joint. The traditional method for pegging a mortise-and-tenon joint is to drive a *square* peg in a *round* hole.

This method works much better than using round pegs or dowels. The corners of the square pegs wedge themselves in the holes and can't work loose.

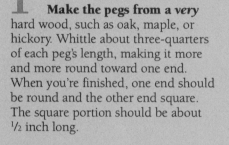

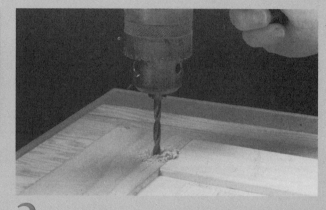

1 **Make the pegs from a *very*** hard wood, such as oak, maple, or hickory. Whittle about three-quarters of each peg's length, making it more and more round toward one end. When you're finished, one end should be round and the other end square. The square portion should be about ½ inch long.

2 **After assembling the joint,** drill one or more holes, as big around as the peg is square, through both the mortise and tenon. **Note:** Don't locate the holes too close to the end of the tenon. The tenon might split when you install the pegs.

3 **Coat each peg with glue and** drive it into the hole, round end first. Tap it in until the square top is almost flush with the surface of the wood. Be careful not to hit the peg so hard that it splinters.

4 **If the rounded portion of a** peg protrudes from the back of the assembly, cut it flush with the surface of the wood. Lightly sand both the round end and the square end.

6

INTERLOCKING JOINTS

Just as most craftsmen consider mortises and tenons the best choice for connecting rails to stiles, legs to aprons, and for other *frame joinery,* they favor interlocking joints for assembling the sides of boxes, drawers, and chests — what is commonly referred to as *box joinery.* There is an important difference between these two types of joinery. Mortises and tenons join boards whose wood grain is oriented to shrink and swell in different directions. Interlocking joints, on the other hand, connect boards that move *in unison.*

This unity of movement allows you to cut intricate mating surfaces when making interlocking joints. Frame joinery is often very plain; if it were too elaborate, gaps would open up between the adjoining members as they expanded and contracted. This, in turn, would weaken the structure. But box joinery, such as dovetails and finger joints, can be as fancy as you want to make it. Consequently, many interlocking joints are both decorative and practical.

INCREASING GLUING SURFACE

Interlocking joints include various types of dovetail joints, finger joints, and lock joints, all of which require multiple cuts. (*SEE FIGURE 6-1.*) The common purpose of these joints is to increase the gluing surface in a corner joint. The mating surfaces of simple corner joints (butt joints, miter joints, and rabbet joints) are relatively small. Often, there are no long-grain-to-long-grain surfaces, just end-grain-to-long-grain and end-grain-to-end-grain. These circumstances combine to make a weak joint. The multiple cuts in an interlocking joint multiply the surface area and often provide a healthy measure of long-grain-to-long-grain gluing surface.

Despite these multiple cuts, interlocking joints are not difficult to make. It's the *number* of cuts that cause an interlocking joint to look intricate, not the *complexity* of the cuts. Most joints require just one or two simple cuts that are repeated over and over again. As long as your layout and setup are accurate, the actual cutting will prove very easy.

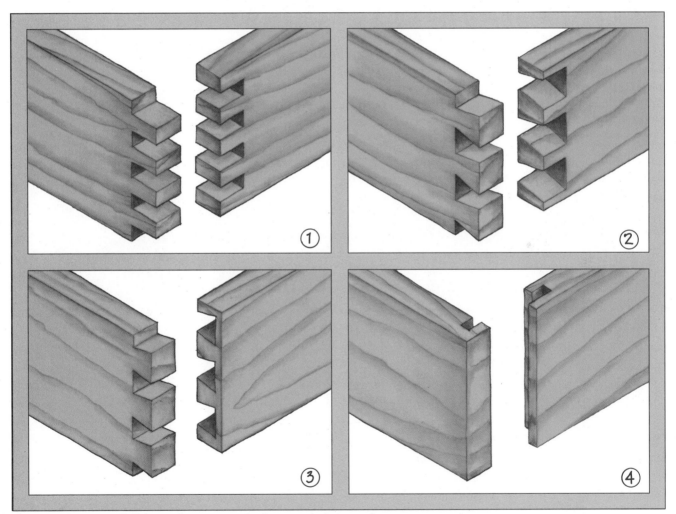

6-1 Of the many different types of interlocking joints, here are four of the most common: A *finger joint* (1), also referred to as a "box joint," is used to join the corners of boxes. A *through dovetail joint* (2) joins boxes, chests, and the rear corners of drawers. A *half-blind dovetail* (3), which can only be seen from one direction, is often used to join the *front* corners of drawers. A *lock joint* (4), also called a tongue-and-dado joint, is another joint that can only be seen from one side. It's often used to join the corners of drawers, especially small ones.

FINGER JOINTS

Finger joints are interlocking notches cut into the ends of adjoining boards. Usually, the notches are spaced evenly and they are all the same width. You can cut all the notches in both of the adjoining parts with a single setup, using a miter gauge and the "Finger-Joint Jig" shown on page 84.

The jig is designed to work on either a table saw with a dado cutter accessory, or a router table with a straight bit. You'll find that it's easier to make all sizes of finger joints on a table saw. It's simple enough to make small finger joints in thin stock on a router table, but the procedure becomes progressively more time consuming as the fingers grow wider and the stock gets thicker. Remember, routers are designed to remove only small amounts of stock at one time.

When making finger joints, the setup is critical. The width of the stop on the jig, the width of the cutter, and the distance between them must all be *precisely* equal. Plan to make several test joints to fine-tune the setup before you cut good stock. (*SEE FIGURES 6-2 THROUGH 6-6.*)

Here are several additional tips:

■ The width of the adjoining boards should be a *multiple* of the finger width. For example, if the fingers are 1/2 inch wide, the adjoining parts might be 5 inches, 5 1/2 inches, or 6 inches wide, but *not* 5 1/4 inches or 5 7/8 inches. If you can't divide the finger width into the board width evenly, you'll end up with partial fingers on one side of each board.

■ The fingers should be *at least* as long as the width of the adjoining board. To be certain that they are long enough, cut them about 1/32 inch longer than needed so they protrude slightly when the joint is assembled. Later, you can sand them flush with the wood surface.

■ Scribe the base of the fingers with a marking gauge — this will help prevent the bit or cutter from tearing the wood grain.

■ As you cut each board, back it up with a scrap. This too will prevent tear-out.

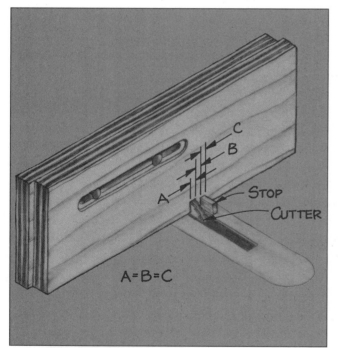

6-2 When setting up to cut finger joints, make sure the width of the stop and the width of the cutter are *precisely* the same. Slide the face of the "Finger-Joint Jig" on page 84 to one side or the other until the distance between the stop and the cutter is equal to the other two dimensions.

6-3 Place the first adjoining board end down against the face of the jig and slide it to one side until the edge butts against the stop. Clamp the board to the jig to prevent it from moving. Turn the saw on and slide the board forward, cutting the first notch. **Note:** To prevent tear-out, always back up the board with a scrap.

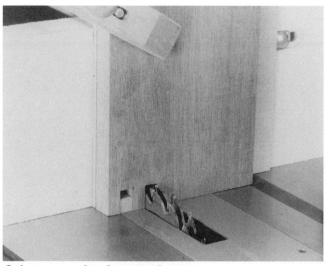

6-4 Loosen the clamp and move the board sideways until the notch you just cut fits over the stop. (It should fit snug, with no perceptible slop.) Tighten the clamp and cut another notch. Repeat until you have cut all the notches in the first adjoining board.

6-5 To cut the first notch in the second adjoining board, use the first board as a spacer. Turn the first board edge for edge and place the first notch over the stop. The first finger should fit between the stop and the cutter. Place the second adjoining board against the jig and slide it sideways until it butts against the first board. Clamp both boards to the jig and cut a notch. The first cut in the second board should create a *corner* notch.

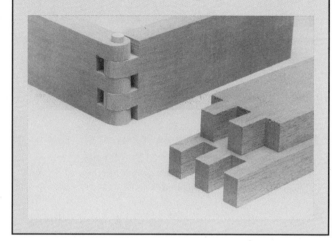

TRY THIS TRICK

To make a wooden hinge, round-over the ends of two boards with a router and a roundover bit. (The radius of this bit must be precisely *half* the thickness of the boards.) Cut finger joints in the rounded ends and assemble the joint. At the center of the rounded ends, drill a hole through the interlocking fingers. Insert a wooden or metal rod in this hole to serve as a pivot.

6-6 Continue cutting notches in the second board in the same manner that you cut them in the first. When you fit the boards together, the fingers and notches should interlock, and the edges of both boards should be flush. If the joint is too *tight,* move the stop *toward* the dado cutter slightly. If it's too *loose,* move it *away.*

Finger-Joint Jig

This jig will evenly space notches as you cut them, allowing you to make finger joints. It's designed to mount on any miter gauge, and will work on both a table saw and a router table. Make the face and the mount from cabinet-grade plywood, and the stop from hardwood. If you wish, make several different faces, each with a different size stop. This will enable you to cut different sizes of finger joints.

To use the jig, screw or bolt the mount to a miter gauge. Loosen the wing nuts that secure the face to the mount and slide the face sideways until the stop is the proper distance away from the bit or cutter. When the stop is positioned properly, tighten the wing nuts.

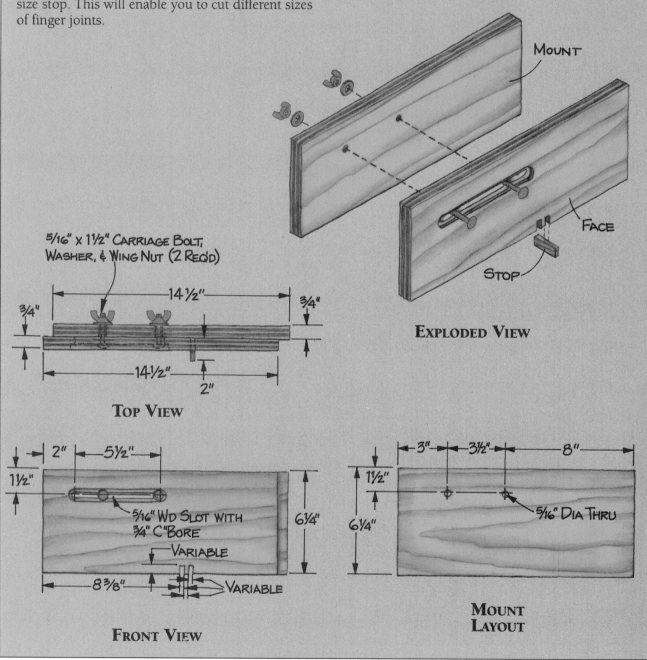

EXPLODED VIEW

TOP VIEW

FRONT VIEW

MOUNT LAYOUT

THROUGH-DOVETAIL JOINTS

Through-dovetail joints have fascinated and frustrated woodworkers for ages. Although there are several different ways to cut them with power tools, no one has yet developed a machine or a fixture to make "classic" dovetail joints — the wide, graceful tails and narrow, delicate pins that have become the hallmark of fine, hand-built furniture. (*See Figure 6-7.*) Careful, patient handwork with a chisel and a dovetail saw remains the only way to make this joint. (*See Figures 6-8 through 6-18.*)

However, there are several simple jigs that will help you through this handwork — the *Layout Rule, Slope Gauge,* and *Chisel Guide.* You'll find the plans for all three of these jigs in "Dovetail Aids" on page 90.

Before making a dovetail joint, decide which part to cut first — the pins or the tails. Craftsmen will argue the point at great length. I prefer to make the tails first, then use these as a template to mark the pins. (I find it more difficult to use the pins to mark the tails.) Here are several additional tips:

■ Make sure that your chisels are razor sharp. Some craftsmen keep a set of finely honed chisels that they use *only* for making dovetail joints.

■ Choose clear, straight-grained wood for the members. It's very difficult to hand cut dovetail joints in figured wood. Also, the grain must run lengthwise through the pins and tails.

■ When you lay out the pins and tails, clearly mark the waste so you don't accidentally remove the wrong part of the board.

■ Keep the slope of the pins and tails between 8 and 12 degrees. If the slope is less than 8 degrees, the pins won't remain wedged between the tails as firmly as they should when the joint is subjected to racking stress. If it's more than 12 degrees, the cheeks of the tails become fragile and will shear off. This makes the joint more susceptible to shear stress.

■ Always cut on the *waste* side of the layout lines. This will ensure that the joints fit tightly. It's much easier to shave a little stock from the pins of a dovetail joint that fits too tight than it is to shim the pins of a loose joint.

■ Make both the pins and the tails about $1/32$ inch longer than the thickness of the adjoining boards. After assembling the joint, sand the outside surfaces flush.

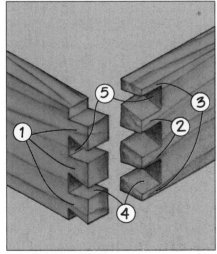

6-7 All dovetail joints consist of two parts. The *tails* (1) are cut into one of the adjoining members, and the mating *pins* (2) are cut into the other. Traditionally, dovetail joints have split pins or *half pins* (3) at the top and bottom edge — tails are not usually split. Each of the tails, pins, and half pins are tiny tenons with angled *cheeks* (4) and square *shoulders* (5).

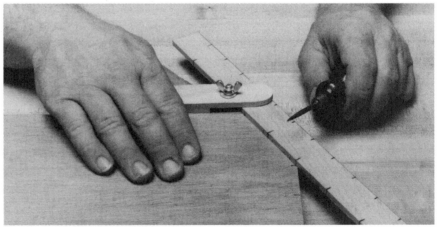

6-8 To make a through-dovetail joint — or *any* dovetail joint — first mark the spacing of the dovetails. Decide how many tails you want to cut across the width of the tail board. For example, if you want to cut five dovetails (five tails and six pins) across the board, hold the *Layout Rule* (see page 90) at an angle, using five spaces — no more, no less — to span the width. (For small dovetails, use the edge on which the lines are 1 inch apart; for larger dovetails, use the side on which the lines are 1½ inches apart.) Place the holder against one edge of the board and slip it onto the rule, gripping the rule at the proper angle. Keeping the holder against the board's edge, slide the rule toward the end of the board. Where each line on the rule crosses the end, make a mark on the board. When you're finished, there should be four marks on the end of the board, dividing its width into five equal sections.

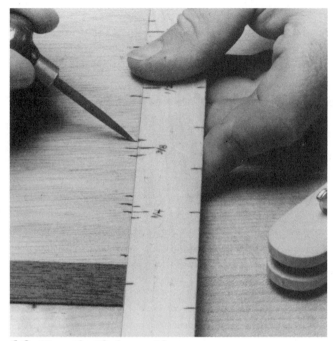

6-9 Next, decide how wide to make the pins. The narrowest part of the pin — the side that will be flush with the outside of the assembled joint — must be *at least* as wide as your smallest paring chisel. Using the special marks on the *Layout Rule* that indicate pin width, mark the narrow sides of the pins at each of the spacing marks, as shown. Remember to mark *half* pins at the top and bottom edges of the board. Using a small square, transfer these marks to *both* sides of the board.

6-10 Using a marking gauge, scribe the base of the tails on both sides and both edges of the board. Be sure to set the marking gauge for $1/32$ inch more than the wood thickness, as mentioned previously.

6-11 Mark the angled cheeks of the tails with the *Slope Gauge* (see page 90), scribing angled lines from the baseline to the marks that indicate the width of the pins. Mark all the right-sloping cheeks, then turn the gauge over and mark the left-sloping cheeks. Remember to mark *both* sides of the board. Shade the stock between the tails to indicate the waste.

6-12 Using a dovetail saw or a dozuki saw, cut the sloping cheeks down to the baseline. If you wish, use the *Slope Gauge* as shown to help start the cut. You can also use the *Chisel Guide* (see page 90) to hold the board as you cut it.

6-13 As you cut the cheeks, you must monitor *both* sides of the board, making sure the saw follows both sets of layout lines. You can do this with a great deal of head bobbing, *or* you can use the *Third Eye* (see page 31) to keep watch on the side of the board facing away from you.

6-14 Once you've cut the cheeks of the tails, cut along the baseline to remove the waste. Do this with a chisel, using it alternately as a cutting tool and a wedge. Clamp the board in the *Chisel Guide,* aligning the guide block with the base layout line. Place the chisel so the edge is on the layout line and the back is flat against the guide block — this will hold the chisel vertically at precisely 90 degrees to the surface of the stock. Strike the chisel lightly with a mallet, cutting through the grain and about $1/16$ inch into the wood.

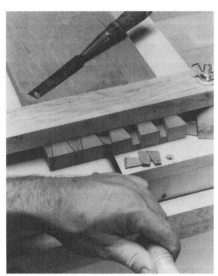

6-15 Next, split out a bit of the
waste. Hold the chisel horizontally
with its edge against the end and
about $1/16$ inch below the surface.
Again, strike the chisel lightly with a
mallet. This time, it will split out a
small amount of waste. Continue cutting and splitting with the chisel
until you have removed the waste
halfway through the board. Turn the
board over and repeat, removing the
remaining waste.

6-16 After cutting the tails,
scribe the base of the pins with a
marking gauge. (Once again, the
pins should be $1/32$ inch longer than
the thickness of the adjoining board.)
Then use the tails as a template to
mark the cheeks of the pins. Clamp
the pin board *vertically* in the *Chisel
Guide* and the tail board *horizontally*.
The tails should cover the end of the

pin board and the surfaces should be
flush, as shown. Place the back of a
chisel against one of the sloping
cheeks of the tails. Tap the chisel
with a mallet, cutting about $1/32$ inch
into the end of the pin board. Repeat
for all the cheeks of all the tails.
Remove the board from the *Chisel
Guide* and shade the waste between
the pins.

6-17 Cut the cheeks of the pins
with a dovetail saw or a dozuki saw.
As you did when making the tails,
you can use the *Slope Gauge* to start
the cut, and the *Third Eye* to monitor
the underside of the board as the cut
progresses.

6-18 After cutting the cheeks of
the pins, clamp the pin board in the
Chisel Guide, aligning the guide
block with the base layout line.
Remove the waste between the pins
as you did with the tails, using the
chisel alternately as a cutting tool

and a wedge. When the waste is
gone, fit the joint together. The pins
should slide easily between the tails,
and the edges of the board should be
flush. Sand the protruding ends
flush after the joint is assembled.

Probably the most difficult step in making through-dovetail joints is sawing the cheeks of the pins and tails. For this reason, some craftsmen prefer to do this operation with a power tool, even though they perform all the remaining work by hand. You have two choices — a table saw or a band saw. If you use a table saw, adjust the *blade* to cut the *tails,* and the *miter gauge* to cut the *pins. (SEE FIGURE 6-19.)* If you use a band saw, you won't have to adjust anything to cut the tails, but you'll need to make an auxiliary table to cut the pins. *(SEE FIGURE 6-20.)*

6-19 If you would rather use a power tool to do the sawing, you can cut the cheeks of the pins and tails on a table saw with an ordinary saw blade. Tilt the blade to cut the tails, adjusting the angle to match the slope of the cheeks. Cut all the cheeks that lean in one direction, using a miter gauge with an extension face to guide the stock. Turn the board edge for edge and cut the remaining cheeks. The procedure for cutting the pins is similar, but you must angle the miter gauge instead of tilting the blade.

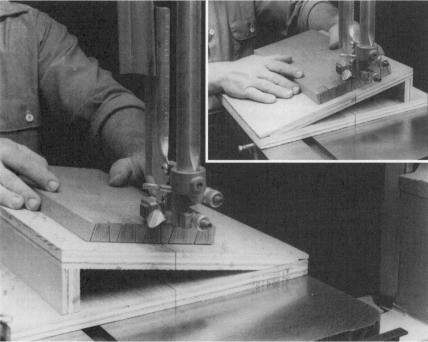

6-20 You can also do the cutting on a bandsaw. You don't have to adjust anything to cut the cheeks of the tails; just follow the layout lines. To cut the pins, you must make a tilted auxiliary worktable, since the tilt of a typical band saw table is limited in one direction. If you make the reversible worktable shown, you can use it to cut both the right-sloping and left-sloping pin cheeks. This will ensure that all the slopes match exactly. **Note:** If you need to adjust the slope of a pin cheek *slightly* to match an adjoining tail, tilt the band saw table. Although the tilt may be limited in one direction, you should be able to alter it at least 2 or 3 degrees.

DOVETAIL AIDS

Here are three easy-to-make jigs that will greatly simplify the task of making hand-cut dovetail joints — a *Layout Rule*, a *Chisel Guide*, and a *Slope Gauge*.

Layout Rule — The rule and holder are used in the same manner as a sliding T-bevel. The rule is marked so you can space the tails evenly *and* measure the width of the pins. Cut all the parts from hardwood and mark the rule with an awl, indelible ink, or a woodburning tool. Glue the parts of the holder together. Insert the bolt and tighten the nut until the holder will grasp the rule firmly, but not so firmly that the rule becomes immobile.

Chisel Guide — The guide holds the boards while you remove the waste from between the pins

and tails. It also directs the chisel and will keep both boards in proper alignment while you use the tail board to lay out the pin board. Make the guide blocks from hardwood and the horizontal and vertical bases from cabinet-grade plywood. Glue *and* screw the bases together.

Slope Gauge — This gauge not only marks the slope of the tails and pins, but it will also guide a saw when you start a cut. Before making the gauge, decide on the slope — it should be between 8 and 12 degrees for the joint to be as strong as possible. Cut the parts from hardwood and glue them together. The edges of the ledgers must be precisely parallel.

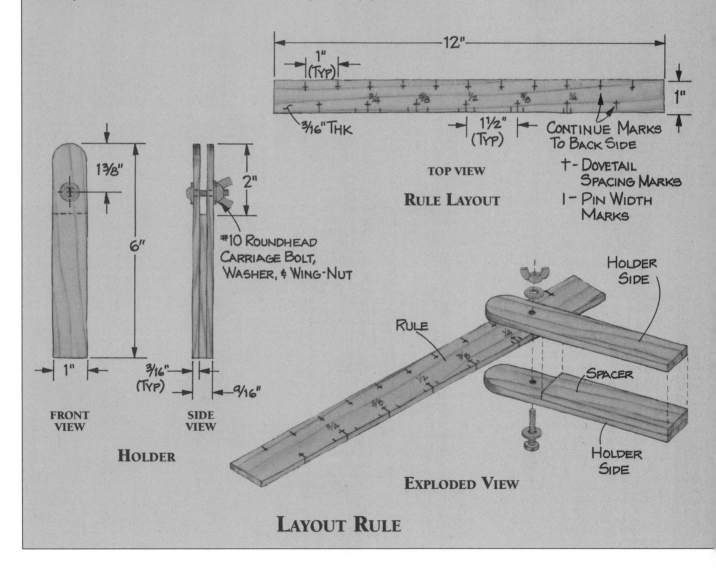

LAYOUT RULE

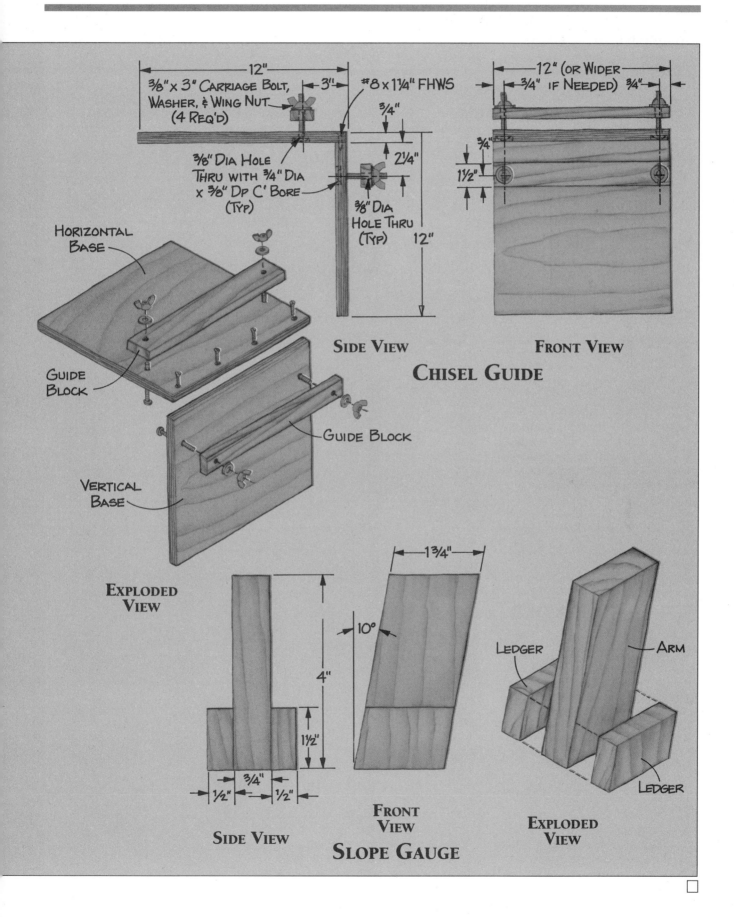

12"

3/8" x 3" Carriage Bolt, Washer, & Wing Nut (4 Req'd)

3"

#8 x 1¼" FHWS

3/8" Dia Hole Thru with ¾" Dia x 3/8" Dp C' Bore (Typ)

3/8" Dia Hole Thru (Typ)

¾"

2¼"

12"

12" (or Wider if Needed)

¾"

¾"

¾"

1½"

SIDE VIEW

FRONT VIEW

CHISEL GUIDE

HORIZONTAL BASE

GUIDE BLOCK

GUIDE BLOCK

VERTICAL BASE

EXPLODED VIEW

1¾"

10°

4"

1½"

½"

¾"

½"

LEDGER

ARM

LEDGER

EXPLODED VIEW

SIDE VIEW

FRONT VIEW

SLOPE GAUGE

HALF-BLIND DOVETAILS

Making half-blind dovetails is similar to making through dovetails. You can use the same jigs for layout and cutting. However, there are two important differences:

■ The length of the tails should be no less than one half the thickness of the pin board, but no more than three quarters.

■ The notches between the pins must all be cut blind, so you can't see the ends of the tails when the joint is assembled.

Make the tails first, following the same procedures shown in the previous section. (*SEE FIGURES 6-7 THROUGH 6-15.*) However, you must alter the technique when making the pins. Instead of sawing the cheeks and removing the waste with a chisel, cut the cheeks only partway. Remove as much waste as you can with a drill, then cut away the remaining waste with a chisel. (*SEE FIGURES 6-21 THROUGH 6-23.*)

6-21 When making the pins of a half-blind dovetail joint, cut the cheeks only *partway* with the saw. Stop cutting when the saw reaches the base of the pins on the *face* of the board, and the bottom of the notches on the *end.*

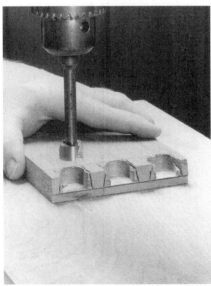

6-22 Remove as much waste as possible from each notch by drilling it out with a Forstner bit. Stop when the bit reaches the bottom of the notch.

6-23 Remove the remaining waste and finish cutting the pin cheeks with a chisel. As shown previously, use the chisel alternately as a cutting tool and a wedge, cutting down through the grain, then splitting out a small amount of waste.

When removing the waste from between the pins of half-blind dovetails, it's difficult to reach into the corners with ordinary paring chisels. Purchase two extra ½-inch chisels and regrind the cutting edges so each chisel has a 15-degree *skew*. One chisel should skew to the right, and the other to the left. This will enable you to reach into the corners on *both* sides of each notch. **Note:** Some woodworkers prefer to use a woodcarver's skew chisel or a miniature lathe turner's skew chisel for this task.

LOCK JOINTS

Like half-blind dovetail joints, lock joints (or locking tongue-and-dado joints) cannot be seen from one direction, and are often used to assemble drawers. They are much easier to make than dovetails — you can cut them with a single setup on a table saw. The trade-off is that they don't withstand shear stress as well as dovetail joints — the wood in front of the dado will shear off if you pull too hard on the drawer front. However, they are still a good choice for small drawers or drawers that won't see much use.

To make a lock joint, mount a dado cutter on a table saw and adjust the depth of cut to equal the thickness of the board. Make a spacer that you can lay over the cutter to quickly reduce the depth of cut.

Using the fence to guide the stock — and without the spacer in place — cut a deep groove in the end of one adjoining board. This groove will create two long tongues. Put the spacer in place and cut the inside tongue short. Then, with the spacer still in place, cut a shallow dado near the end of the other adjoining board. The tongue should fit snugly in the dado. (*SEE FIGURES 6-24 THROUGH 6-27.*)

Note: As shown, this procedure will create a lock joint in two ¾-inch-thick boards. To join thinner or thicker boards, you must change the width of the dado cutter, the thickness of the spacer, and the location of the fence.

6-24 To make a lock joint in ¾-inch-thick stock, mount a dado cutter on your table saw and adjust it to make a ¼-inch-wide cut. Adjust the depth of cut to ¾ inch. Position the fence precisely ¼ inch away from the cutter. From a ½-inch-thick scrap of plywood or hardboard, make a spacer that will fit over the cutter and against the fence, as shown.

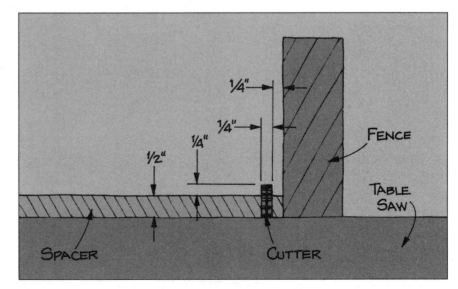

6-25 *Without* **the spacer in place,** cut a ¼-inch-wide, ¾-inch-deep groove in the end of one adjoining board. Hold the stock vertically, and use a square scrap of plywood to help guide the stock along the fence. This cut will create two ¼-inch-thick, ¾-inch-long tongues on the end of the board.

6-26 **Put the spacer in place,** clamping it to the work surface of the table saw. Holding the stock horizontally with the end against the fence, cut the inside tenon short. Again, use a square scrap of plywood to guide the stock. After making the cut, the short tenon should be just ¼ inch long.

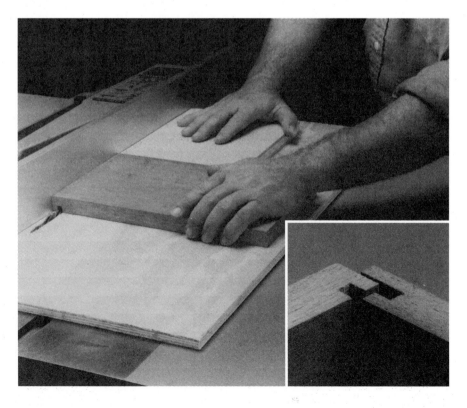

6-27 **Leave the spacer in place** and cut a ¼-inch-wide, ¼-inch-deep dado in the other adjoining board. As you make the cut, hold the board horizontally with the end against the fence. Again, use the scrap of plywood to guide the stock. When the parts are assembled, the short tongue will fit the dado.

PROJECTS

7

PEWTER RACK

In days gone by, dishes and other eating utensils were often made from pewter. Hanging shelves such as these were called "pewter racks," since they were designed to store the metal utensils. The edges of dishes and plates fit in grooves in the shelves and rested against plate rails at the back of the unit. Cups and small bowls rested on the shelves in front of the plates. Spoons and forks hung in notches in the front edges of the shelves.

The joinery in the project is very basic. The shelves are joined to the sides with blind dadoes and rabbets. The braces, valance, and rails are notched into the sides. And the molding is attached to the valance with glue blocks.

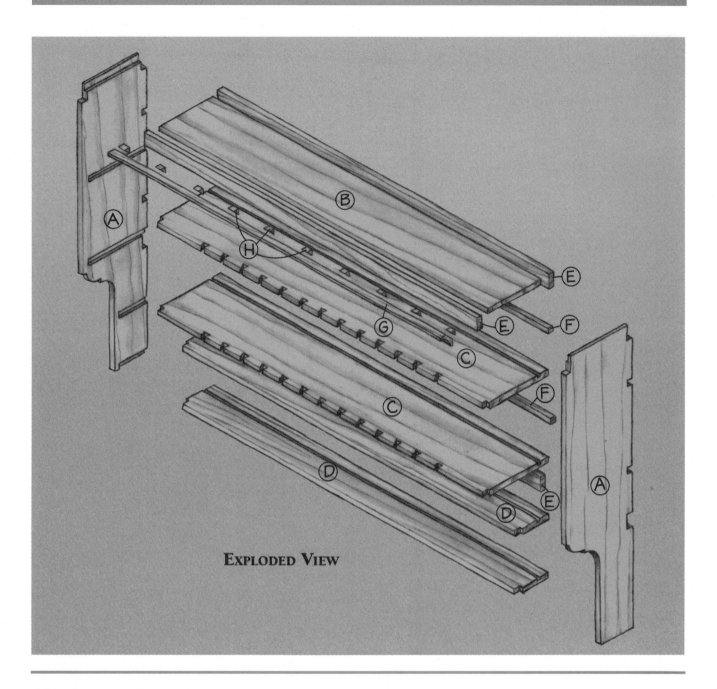

EXPLODED VIEW

MATERIALS LIST (FINISHED DIMENSIONS)

Parts

A. Sides (2)   ³/₄″ x 10″ x 42″
B. Top   ³/₄″ x 8¹/₂″ x 50³/₄″
C. Wide
   shelves (3)   ³/₄″ x 10″ x 50³/₄″
D. Narrow
   shelves (2)   ³/₄″ x 5″ x 50³/₄″
E. Braces/
   valance (3)   ³/₄″ x 2″ x 51¹/₂″

F. Plate
   rails (2)   ³/₄″ x ³/₄″ x 51¹/₂″
G. Cove
   molding   ³/₄″ x 2¹/₈″ x 51¹/₂″
H. Glue blocks (10) ³/₄″ x 1″ x 1″

Hardware

#8 x 1¹/₄″ Flathead wood screws
(36–42)

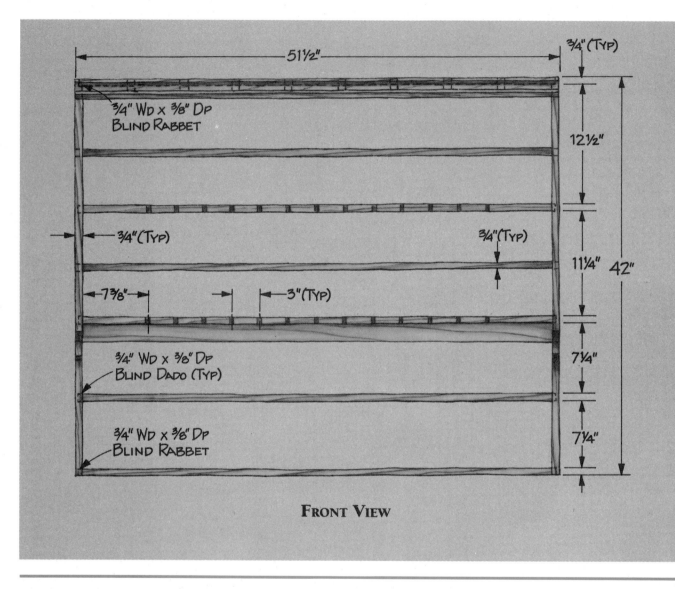

3/4" (TYP)

51½"

3/4" WD x 3/8" DP
BLIND RABBET

12½"

3/4" (TYP)

3/4" (TYP)

11¼"   42"

7⅜"   3" (TYP)

3/4" WD x 3/8" DP
BLIND DADO (TYP)

7¼"

3/4" WD x 3/8" DP
BLIND RABBET

7¼"

FRONT VIEW

PLAN OF PROCEDURE

1 Select the stock and cut the parts to size.
To make this project, you need about 31 board feet of
4/4 (four-quarters) lumber. The pewter rack shown is
made from poplar, but you can use any cabinet-grade
hardwood.

Plane the 4/4 lumber to ¾ inch thick and cut the
parts to the sizes shown in the Materials List *except*
the cove molding. Make this about ½ inch wider and
4 inches longer than specified.

2 Cut the joinery in the sides. The shelves rest
in blind dadoes and rabbets in the sides, and the
valance, braces, and plate rails rest in notches. Lay
out these joints as shown in the *Front View* and *Side*

View. Cut the dadoes and rabbets with a router, then
square the blind ends with a chisel. Cut the notches
with a band saw or saber saw.

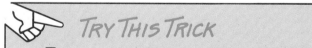

TRY THIS TRICK

To save time, fasten the sides together with
double-faced carpet tape. Cut the notches in *both*
boards at the same time, then separate the boards
and discard the tape. **Note:** You can also use this
technique to cut the side shapes, shelving corner
notches, and shelving dovetail notches.

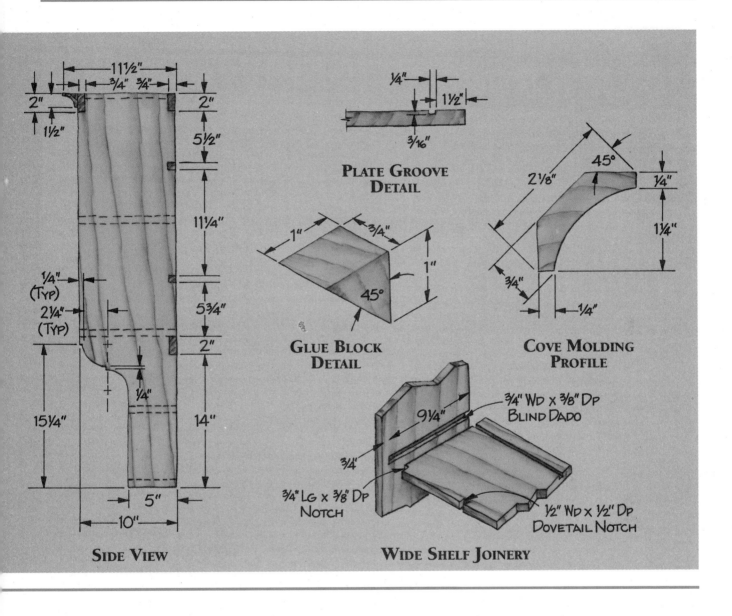

PLATE GROOVE DETAIL

GLUE BLOCK DETAIL

COVE MOLDING PROFILE

SIDE VIEW

WIDE SHELF JOINERY

3/4" WD x 3/8" DP BLIND DADO

3/4" LG x 3/8" DP NOTCH

1/2" WD x 1/2" DP DOVETAIL NOTCH

3 Cut the shape of the sides. Lay out the shape of the sides as shown in the *Side View.* Cut the shapes with a band saw or saber saw, then sand the sawed edges.

4 Cut the notches in the ends of the shelves. The front corners of the shelves are notched to fit the blind dadoes and rabbets. Cut these notches with a saber saw or dovetail saw.

5 Cut the plate grooves in the wide shelves. The wide shelves are grooved near the back edge, as shown in the *Plate Groove Detail.* These grooves hold plates vertically so they rest against the plate rails.

Cut the 1/4-inch-wide, 3/16-inch-deep plate grooves with a router or a dado cutter.

6 Cut the dovetail notches in the wide shelves. The front edges of the wide shelves are notched to hold forks and spoons. Cut these notches on a table-mounted router with a dovetail bit. Use a miter gauge to guide the stock over the bit. (*See Figure 7-1.*)

7 Make the cove molding. The valance is decorated with a simple cove molding. To make this molding, double-bevel both edges of the molding stock with the saw blade tilted at 45 degrees, as shown in the *Cove Molding Profile.* Cut the cove in the front face by passing the stock across the table saw at an angle. (SEE FIGURE 7-2.) Scrape and sand the sawed surfaces smooth.

8 **Assemble the pewter rack.** Dry assemble the rack (*without* glue) to check the fit of the joints. Finish sand all the parts, then reassemble the shelves, braces, and valance with glue. Reinforce the glue joints with flathead wood screws. Counterbore *and* countersink the screw holes, then cover the heads with wooden plugs. After the glue dries, sand the plugs and joints clean and flush.

Attach the glue blocks to the molding with glue. Let the glue set, then glue the molding assembly to the valance. If you wish, drive a few screws from the back side of the valance into the glue blocks to help hold the molding in place.

9 **Finish the pewter rack.** Do any necessary touch-up sanding to the completed pewter rack, then apply a finish. The project shown has a simulated antique finish. Mix a little water with flat latex paint to thin it slightly. Apply several coats to all wooden surfaces. Let the paint dry completely (at least 24 hours), lightly sand the surface with very fine sandpaper (220-grit or finer), and apply a coat of boiled linseed oil. This will reproduce the look and feel of an old-time milk paint finish.

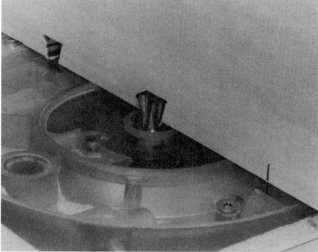

7-1 **Cut the silverware notches** in the front edge of the wide shelves with a table-mounted router and a dovetail bit. Fasten the shelves face to face with double-faced carpet tape, then cut all three boards at once.

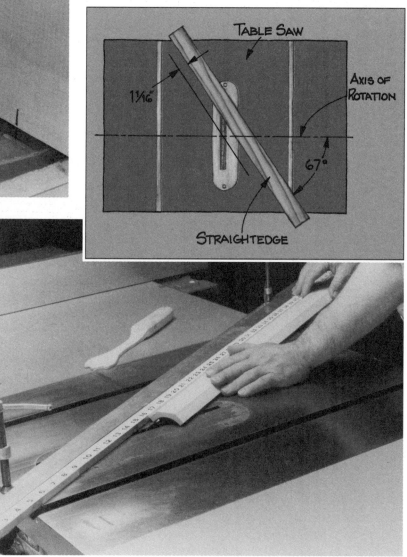

7-2 **To cut the cove in the** molding, pass the stock over the saw blade at an angle. Clamp a straightedge to the saw to guide the stock. For a standard 10-inch blade, the straightedge should be angled 67 degrees from the axis of rotation, as shown. Lower the saw blade until it protrudes about $1/16$ inch from the table. Turn the saw on and make the first pass, removing just a little stock. Raise the blade another $1/16$ inch and make another pass. Repeat until the cove is $1/2$ inch deep.

8

MINIATURE CHEST OF DRAWERS

In days gone by, miniature chests of drawers were used to store and transport small items such as important papers, sewing notions, and machinist's tools. The individual drawers separated and organized the items, much like a small, portable filing cabinet. The doors kept the drawers from falling open and spilling the contents when the chest was moved from place to place.

Today, small chests remain as useful as they ever were, although we tend not to move them about as much as our ancestors. The chest shown will hold jewelry, collectibles, stationery, and dozens of small items that fill our lives.

Like many miniature pieces, this chest is made with simpler joinery than you might use in a full-size chest of drawers. Instead of dovetails, the drawers are assembled with lock joints. Instead of web frames, the drawers slide in and out on simple guides set in blind dadoes. And instead of mortises and tenons, the door frames are joined with dowel joints.

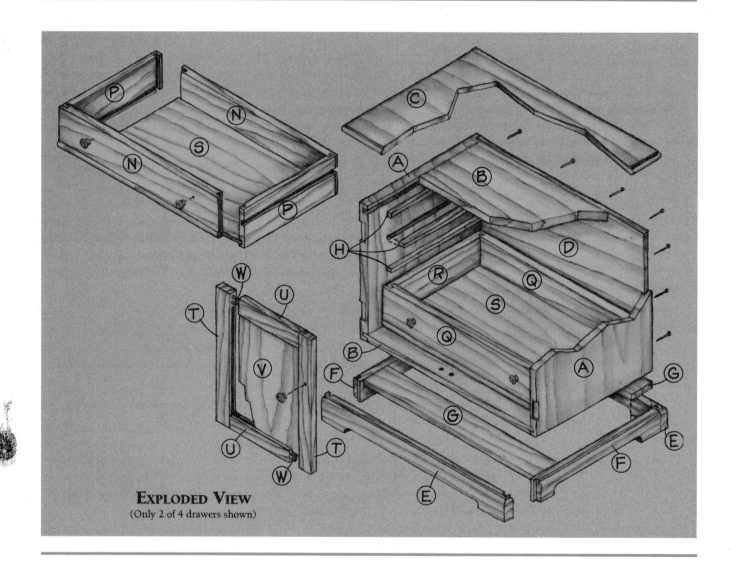

EXPLODED VIEW
(Only 2 of 4 drawers shown)

MATERIALS LIST (FINISHED DIMENSIONS)

Parts

A. Sides (2)   ½" x 9" x 9"

B. Sub-top/
   bottom (2)   ½" x 8¾" x 13"

C. Top   ½" x 10¼" x 14¼"

D. Back   ¼" x 9" x 13"

E. Base front/
   back (2)   ½" x 1¼" x 14¼"

F. Base sides (2)   ½" x 1¼" x 9¾"

G. Ledgers (2)   ½" x 1¾" x 13¼"

H. Drawer
   guides (8)   ¼" x ⁷/₁₆" x 7"

J. Top drawer front/
   back (2)   ⅜" x ³¹/₃₂" x 12⁷/₁₆"

K. Top drawer
   sides (2)   ⅜" x ³¹/₃₂" x 7¼"

L. Top middle drawer front/
   back (2)   ⅜" x 1³¹/₃₂" x 12⁷/₁₆"

M. Top middle drawer
   sides (2)   ⅜" x 1³¹/₃₂" x 7¼"

N. Bottom middle drawer front/
   back (2)   ⅜" x 2⁷/₃₂" x 12⁷/₁₆"

P. Bottom middle drawer
   sides (2)   ⅜" x 2⁷/₃₂" x 7¼"

Q. Bottom drawer front/
   back (2)   ⅜" x 2¹¹/₁₆" x 12⁷/₁₆"

R. Bottom drawer
   sides (2)   ⅜" x 2¹¹/₁₆" x 7¼"

S. Drawer
   bottoms* (4) ⅛" x 7" x 11¹⁵/₁₆"

T. Door stiles (4) ½" x 1" x 8¹⁵/₁₆"

U. Door rails (4)   ½" x 1" x 4²³/₃₂"

V. Door
   panels (2)   ¼" x 5⅛" x 7⅜"

W. Dowels (16)   ¼" dia. x 1"

Make these parts from plywood.

Hardware

1" Brads (12–16)

¾" x 1½" Hinges and mounting
   screws (4)

Drawer/door pulls (10)

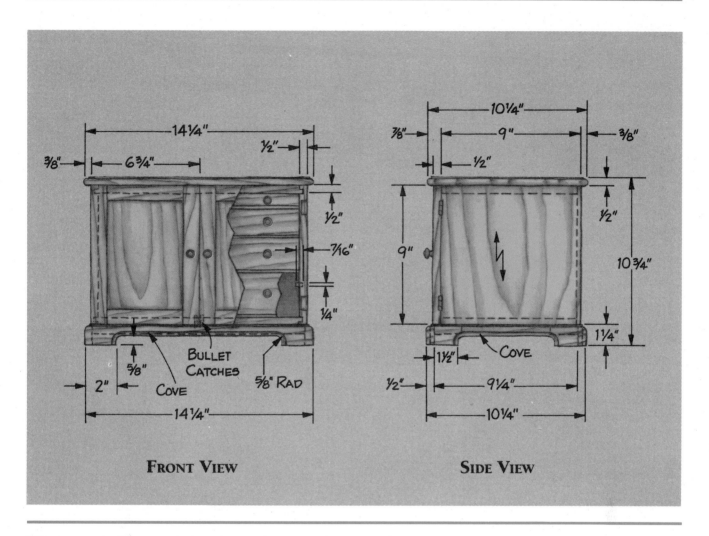

FRONT VIEW

SIDE VIEW

PLAN OF PROCEDURE

1 Select the stock and cut the parts to size. To make this project, you need about 10 board feet of 4/4 (four-quarters) lumber and a few scraps of ⅛-inch plywood. The chest shown is made from cherry, but you can use any cabinet-grade hardwood.

Plane the 4/4 lumber to ½ inch thick, and cut the sides, top, sub-top, bottom, base frame members, ledgers, and door frame members to size. Set some ½-inch-thick stock aside to use for test pieces. Plane the remaining stock to ⅜ inch thick. Set aside enough of this stock to cut the drawer parts, but *don't* make them until after you've assembled the case. Plane the remaining stock to ¼ inch thick, and cut the back, drawer guides, and door panels.

2 Cut the joinery for the case. The case is joined with simple rabbets and dadoes. Make these joints:

■ ¼-inch-wide, ¼-inch-deep rabbets in the back edges of the sides, as shown in the *Side Layout,* to hold the back

■ ¼-inch-wide, ¼-inch-deep rabbets in the ends of the sub-top and bottom to create bare-faced tongues to fit in the sides

■ ¼-inch-wide, ¼-inch-deep dadoes near the top and bottom ends of the sides to hold the sub-top and the bottom

■ ¼-inch-wide, ¼-inch-deep *blind* dadoes in the sides to hold the drawer guides

3 Cut the joinery in the base. The parts of the base are held together with rabbet-and-dado joints. Cut ¼-inch-wide, ¼-inch-deep dadoes in the base front and back, and ¼-inch-wide, ¼-inch-deep rabbets in the ends of the base sides. These rabbets will create bare-faced tongues to fit the dadoes.

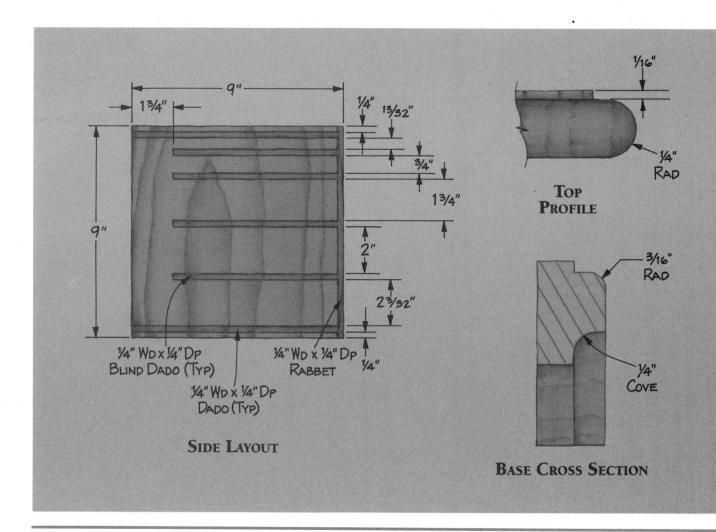

SIDE LAYOUT

TOP PROFILE

BASE CROSS SECTION

4   Cut the shapes of the base parts.   The base front, back, and sides are all cut out to create feet. Lay out the shapes of these cutouts as shown in the *Front View* and *Side View,* then saw them with a band saw or scroll saw. Sand the sawed edges.

5   Shape the top and base parts.   Both the top and the base have decorative edges. Using a router and a ¼-inch radius roundover bit, shape all four edges of the top, as shown in the *Top Profile*. Using a ¼-inch radius cove bit, cut a cove in the base cutouts, as shown in the *Base Cross Section*. Using a ³⁄₁₆-inch bead cutter, cut a quarter bead in the top edges of the base parts.

6   Assemble the case.   Finish sand all the parts of the case you've made so far, being careful not to round-over any adjoining ends or edges. Dry assemble the case (*without* glue) to check the fit of the joints.

Mount the drawer guides in the sides, gluing just the first 2 to 3 inches. Let the glue set, then assemble the sides, sub-top, and bottom with glue. Before the glue dries, fasten the back to the sides, sub-top, and bottom with brads — but do *not* glue it in place. This will let the back expand and contract with changes in humidity. When the glue dries, sand the joints clean and flush.

Glue the base front, back, sides, and ledgers together. Let the glue dry, and sand the joints. Glue the top and base assembly to the case assembly.

7   Assemble the doors.   The door frames are doweled together, and the panels rest in grooves. Cut ¼-inch-wide, ¼-inch-deep grooves in the inside edges of the rails, and *double-blind* ¼-inch-wide, ¼-inch-deep grooves in the inside edges of the stiles. These double-blind grooves should stop ⅝ inch before the ends of the boards.

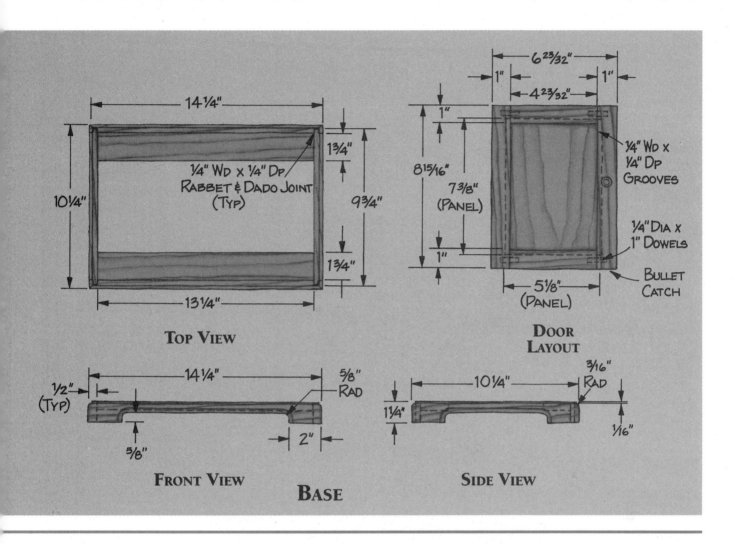

TOP VIEW

DOOR LAYOUT

BASE

FRONT VIEW   **SIDE VIEW**

Drill ¼-inch-diameter, ⁹⁄₁₆-inch-deep dowel holes in the ends of the rails and inside edges of the stiles, as shown in the *Door Layout*. (The precise locations of the dowels are not critical, but there should be one per joint.) Finish sand the door parts, and assemble the rails and stiles with glue and dowels. As you put together the frames, slide the panels into their grooves. Do *not* glue the panels in place; let them float in the grooves.

8 Hang the doors. Cut hinge mortises in the front edges of the sides and the inside faces of the door frames. Attach door pulls to the inside stiles, and bore the bottom ends of these stiles to hold bullet catches. (*SEE FIGURE 8-1.*) Press the bullet catches into the stiles, and hang the doors on their hinges. Carve small recesses in the front ledger and install the striking plates for the catches. (These plates are usually tacked in place with brads.)

8-1 Install bullet catches in the bottom ends of the inside door stiles to hold the doors closed. These simple catches are just metal tubes, each holding a spring and a ball bearing. They're available from most mail-order woodworking suppliers.

9   **Cut the drawer joinery.** Carefully measure the parts of the case. If the dimensions have changed from those shown in the drawings, adjust the sizes of the drawers accordingly. Cut the drawer fronts, backs, and sides from ³⁄₈-inch-thick stock, and make some extra parts to use as test pieces. Cut the drawer bottoms from ¹⁄₈-inch plywood.

As shown on page 93, the drawer lock joints can be cut with a single setup on a table saw. However, when the adjoining parts are this small, it's easier to use a table-mounted router and a spline cutter. (*SEE FIGURES 8-2 THROUGH 8-4.*) Using either of these tools, also cut ¹⁄₈-inch-wide, ¹⁄₈-inch-deep grooves in the inside faces of the drawer parts to hold the bottoms.

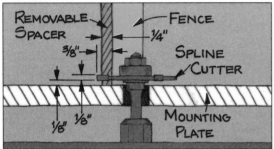

8-2 **Set up the router and the** spline cutter as shown in the inset. Make a ¹⁄₄-inch spacer from plywood or hardboard. First, cut a ¹⁄₈-inch-wide, ³⁄₈-inch deep groove in the ends of each drawer front and back. This groove will create two ¹⁄₈-inch-thick tenons in each end. Do not use the spacer for this step.

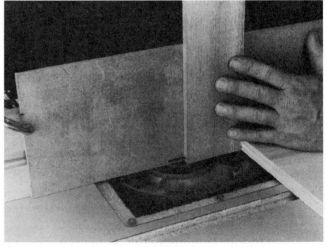

8-3 **Clamp the spacer to the** router table fence. Holding the drawer fronts and backs vertically against the spacer, cut the *inside* tenons so they're just ¹⁄₈ inch long.

8-4 **Finally, cut a ¹⁄₈-inch-wide,** ¹⁄₈″-inch-deep dado in the inside surface of each drawer side, near each end. Again, hold each part vertically as you make the cuts. When you fit the joints together, the short tenons on the drawer fronts and backs should fit the dadoes in the drawer sides.

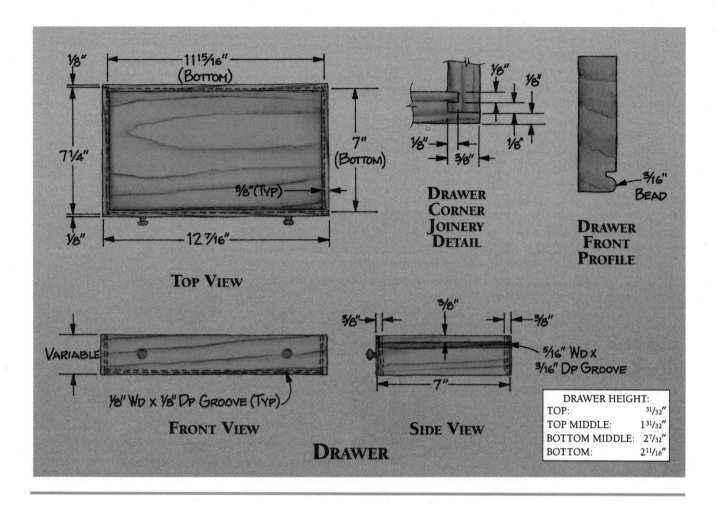

DRAWER

DRAWER HEIGHT:
TOP:	31/32"
TOP MIDDLE:	1 31/32"
BOTTOM MIDDLE:	2 7/32"
BOTTOM:	2 11/16"

10 Cut a bead in the drawer fronts. Using a router and a beading cutter, cut a decorative bead in the bottom edge of the drawer fronts, as shown in the *Drawer Front Profile.* You can also use a molder or a scratch stock to make these beads.

11 Assemble and fit the drawers. Finish sand the drawer parts and assemble the fronts, backs, and sides with glue. As you assemble these parts, slide the drawer bottoms into their grooves but do *not* glue them in place.

Let the glue dry, and sand the joints clean and flush. Using a table-mounted router, cut 5/16-inch-wide, 3/16-inch deep blind grooves in the sides of the assembled drawers. Begin each groove at the back of the drawer, 3/8 inch from the top edge. Cut the groove 7 inches long, stopping before you reach the drawer front, as shown in the *Drawer Side View.*

Attach drawer pulls to the drawer fronts. The precise locations of these pulls are not critical, but they should be evenly spaced. Insert each drawer into the case. If it binds or rubs, remove a little stock from the appropriate part of the drawer with a block plane, scraper, or file. Custom fit each drawer in this manner so it slides smoothly.

12 Finish the chest of drawers. Remove the doors and drawers from the case, and remove the hardware from the doors and drawers. Do any necessary touch-up sanding, then apply a finish to all the surfaces of the case (inside *and* outside), all the surfaces of the doors, and the *outside* surfaces of the drawer fronts. Leave the inside surfaces of the drawers — the parts that won't be seen when the drawers are closed — unfinished. The chest shown was painted with acrylics and sealed with several coats of lacquer.

Let the finish dry, then rub it out to the desired gloss. Rub the drawer guides with paraffin wax to help the drawers slide easily. Replace all the hardware, hang the doors, and insert the drawers in the case.

9

HALF-MOON BENCH

During the early nineteenth-century, the most common form of utility seating was the "five-board" bench — a seat, two legs, and two braces. Shaker craftsmen, with an eye for simplicity and economy, eliminated one of the braces and cut the remaining brace in a graceful half-moon arch. The bench shown here is an adaptation of that Shaker design.

If you have any doubt about the strength of traditional joinery, this project will make a believer out of you. The legs and seat are joined with through dovetails, and the legs and brace with mortises and tenons. All the tenons are wedged to hold tight in the mortises. As a result, this simple bench is incredibly strong and durable.

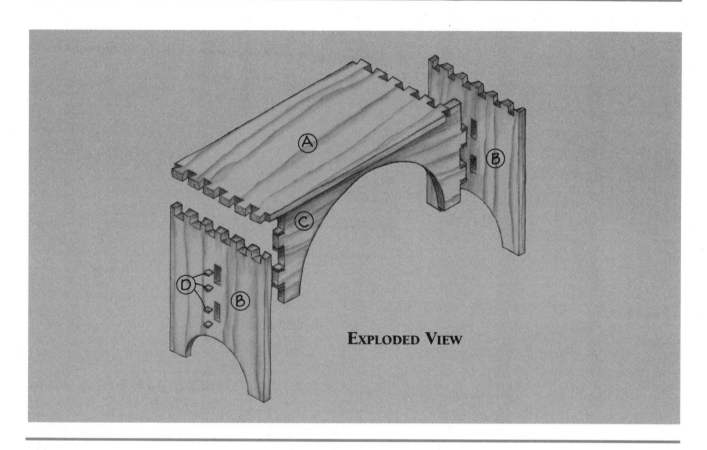

EXPLODED VIEW

MATERIALS LIST (FINISHED DIMENSIONS)

Parts

A. Seat $3/4''$ x 12" x 24"   C. Brace $3/4''$ x $11^{1}/4''$ x 24"
B. Legs (2) $3/4''$ x 12" x 16"   D. Wedges (8) $3/32''$ x $3/4''$ x $3/4''$

PLAN OF PROCEDURE

1 Select the stock and cut the parts to size. To make this project, you need about 8 board feet of 4/4 (four-quarters) lumber. The bench shown is made from walnut and poplar; however, you can use any cabinet-grade wood.

Plane all the 4/4 stock to $3/4$ inch thick. Cut the seat, legs, and brace to the sizes shown in the Materials List, then set the scraps aside to use as test pieces. If the wood is hard enough, you can also use the scraps to make the wedges.

2 Cut the dovetail joints in the legs and seat. The legs and seat are joined by through dovetails. Lay out the tails on both ends of the seat, as shown in the *Dovetail Layout,* and cut them. Using the tails as a template, lay out the pins on the top ends of the legs, then cut them. For step-by-step instructions on how to make through dovetail joints, see page 85.

3 Cut the mortise-and-tenon joints in the legs and brace. The legs are joined to the brace with wedged mortise-and-tenon joints. Lay out the mortises on the legs, as shown in the *End View.* Drill out most of the waste, then clean up the sides and ends with a chisel. Lay out matching tenons on the brace and cut these with a band saw or saber saw.

Cut $1/16$-inch-wide kerfs in the ends of the tenons, as shown in the *Tenon Layout.* At the blind ends of these kerfs, drill $1/8$-inch-diameter holes. These holes will prevent the stock from splitting when you drive the wedges into the tenons. For further instructions on making mortises and tenons, see page 63.

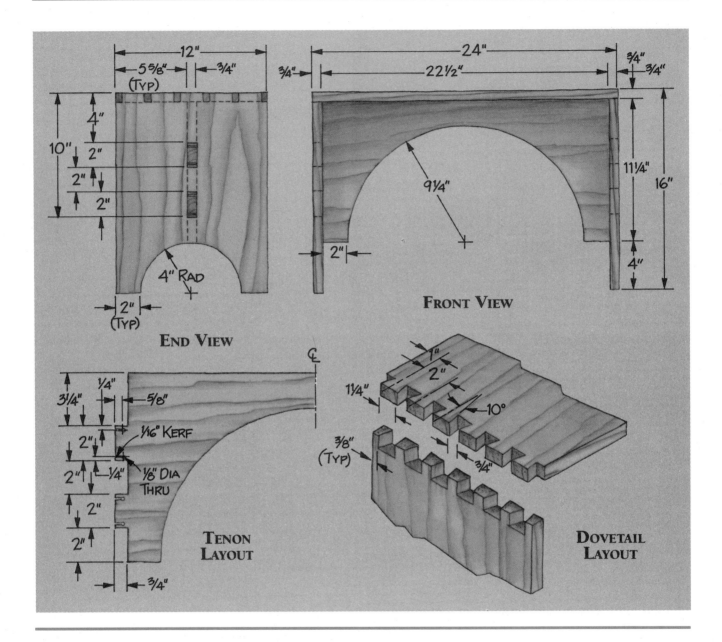

END VIEW

FRONT VIEW

TENON LAYOUT

DOVETAIL LAYOUT

4 Cut the shapes of the legs and brace. Both the legs and the braces have semicircular cutouts. Lay out these shapes on the brace and legs as shown in the *Front View* and *End View*. Make the cutouts with a band saw or saber saw, then sand the sawed edges.

5 Assemble the bench. Finish sand all the parts of the bench, and dry assemble the parts (*without* glue) to check the fit of the joints. From scraps of *very* hard wood (such as maple, oak, or hickory), cut the wedges. These wedges must taper from 3/32 inch thick at one end to a point at the other.

Glue the parts together. Before the glue dries, drive the wedges into the slots in the ends of the tenons. Let the glue dry, then cut the wedges flush with the wood surface. Sand all the joints clean and flush.

6 Finish the bench. Do any necessary touch-up sanding, then apply a finish to the bench. Traditionally, these benches were painted. The bench shown has been finished with tung oil and spar varnish — this mixture makes a clear, durable indoor/outdoor finish. For the first coat, apply straight tung oil. Then mix a cup of tung oil to a tablespoon of varnish, and apply two more coats. Let the finish dry completely, then rub it out with #0000 steel wool and paste wax.

10

CABINETMAKER'S WORKBENCH

A good, solid workbench requires good, solid joinery. The bench shown was designed to provide a stable work surface for heavy use. The leg assemblies are solidly joined with mortises and tenons, and the cabinet parts with interlocking rabbets, dadoes, and grooves. There is no stretcher; instead, the cabinet is joined to the legs to provide a sturdy base for the benchtop.

This arrangement offers some advantages over more traditional designs. The workbench is easier to build and requires fewer materials than a classic cabinetmaker's workbench. But it is just as strong. And since the bench does not require stretchers or other brace work, there is more space for storage. The cabinet provides both drawers and shelves for small and medium-size tools.

You can use the space between the cabinet and the benchtop for frequently used tools. Because this space is open all around the workbench, you have access to these tools from any location. And this open space makes it simple to mount a vise almost anywhere on the benchtop. You can also attach hold-downs and other bench accessories to the benchtop or frame members.

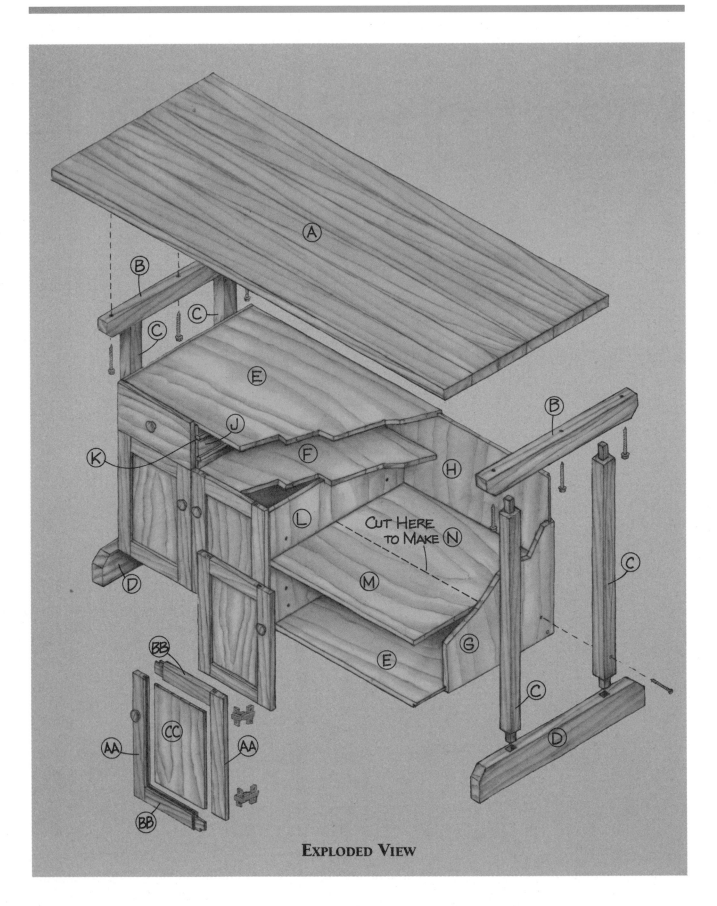

EXPLODED VIEW

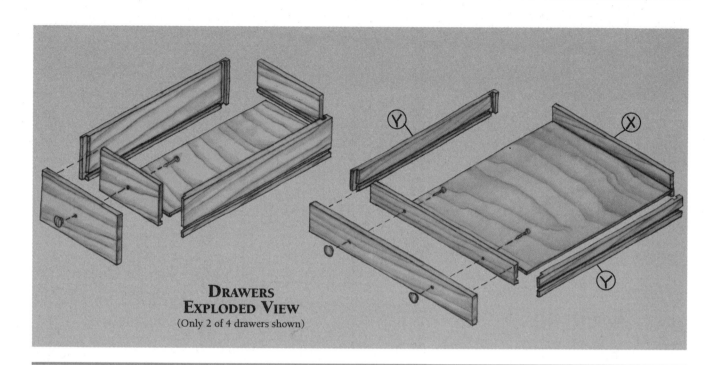

**DRAWERS
EXPLODED VIEW**
(Only 2 of 4 drawers shown)

MATERIALS LIST (FINISHED DIMENSIONS)
Parts

Workbench

A.	Benchtop*	$1^1/2''$ x 25'' x 60''
B.	Top braces (2)	$1^3/4''$ x $2^1/2''$ x 23''
C.	Legs (4)	$1^3/4''$ x $1^3/4''$ x $29^1/2''$
D.	Feet (2)	$1^3/4''$ x $3^1/2''$ x 25''

Cabinet

E.	Case top/bottom/ shelf† (2)	$3/4''$ x $20^1/4''$ x $44^1/4''$
F.	Fixed shelf†	$3/4''$ x $19^1/2''$ x $44^1/4''$
G.	Case sides† (2)	$3/4''$ x $20^1/4''$ x 22''
H.	Case back†	$3/4''$ x $21^1/4''$ x $44^1/4''$
J.	Drawer dividers† (2)	$3/4''$ x 6'' x $19^1/2''$
K.	Drawer guides (8)	$1/2''$ x $1/2''$ x $19^1/2''$
L.	Cupboard divider†	$3/4''$ x $15^1/4''$ x $19^1/2''$
M.	Adjustable shelf†	$3/4''$ x $19^1/4''$ x $21^1/4''$
N.	Adjustable half-shelf†	$3/4''$ x 11'' x $21^1/4''$

Drawers

P.	End drawer faces (2)	$3/4''$ x 6'' x $11^1/4''$
Q.	End drawer fronts/ backs (4)	$1/2''$ x $5^3/16''$ x $9^1/2''$
R.	End drawer sides (4)	$1/2''$ x $5^3/16''$ x $19^1/2''$
S.	End drawer bottoms† (2)	$1/4''$ x $9^1/2''$ x $18^1/2''$
T.	Shallow middle drawer face	$3/4''$ x $2^3/4''$ x $22^1/2''$
U.	Shallow middle drawer front/ back (2)	$1/2''$ x $1^{15}/16''$ x $21^1/8''$
V.	Shallow middle drawer sides (2)	$1/2''$ x $1^{15}/16''$ x $19^1/2''$
W.	Deep middle drawer face	$3/4''$ x $3^1/4''$ x $22^1/2''$
X.	Deep middle drawer front/ back (2)	$1/2''$ x $3^3/16''$ x $21^1/8''$
Y.	Deep middle drawer sides (2)	$1/2''$ x $3^3/16''$ x $19^1/2''$
Z.	Middle drawer bottoms† (2)	$1/4''$ x $18^1/2''$ x $21^1/8''$

Doors

AA.	Stiles (8)	$3/4''$ x 2'' x 16''
BB.	Rails (8)	$3/4''$ x 2'' x $9^3/4''$
CC.	Door panels† (4)	$1/4''$ x 8'' x $12^3/4''$

*This is a standard-size solid maple "butcherblock" countertop, which you can purchase from many lumberyards on special order.
†Make these parts from plywood.

Hardware

$3/8''$ x $3^1/2''$ Lag screws (6)

#8 x $1^1/4''$ Flathead wood screws (48–60)

#12 x 2'' Flathead wood screws (12)

1'' Brads (24–36)

$3/8''$ Flat washers (6)

$1^1/4''$ Drawer/door pulls (10)

European-style full overlay hinges (8)

$1/4''$ dia. Shelving support pins (8)

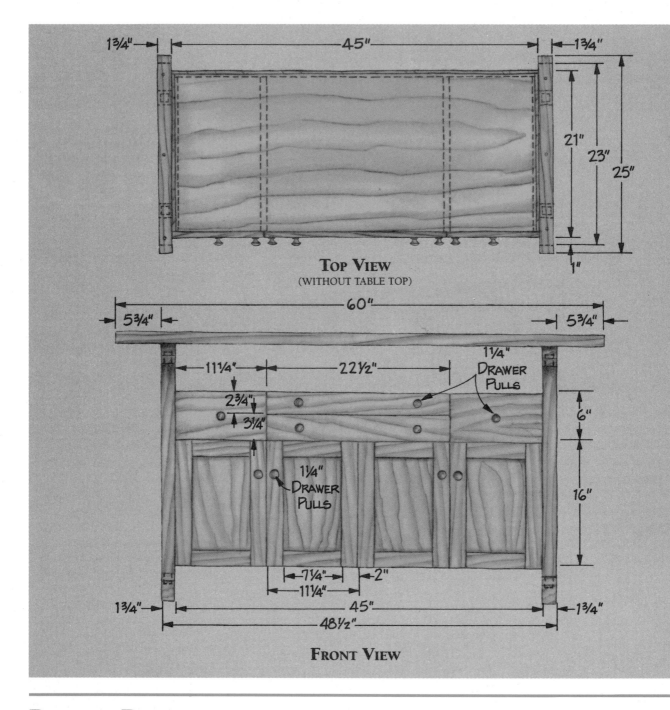

TOP VIEW
(WITHOUT TABLE TOP)

FRONT VIEW

PLAN OF PROCEDURE

1 Select the stock and cut the parts to size. To make this workbench, you need about 34 board feet of 8/4 (eight-quarters) stock, 15 board feet of 4/4 (four-quarters) stock, two 4 x 8-foot sheets of cabinet-grade ³/₄-inch plywood, and one 4 x 4-foot sheet of cabinet-grade ¹/₄-inch plywood. (If you purchase the benchtop ready-made, you'll need only 14 board feet

of 8/4 stock.) All the solid stock should be a hardwood, such as birch, maple, or oak, and the plywood veneer should either match or complement the solid wood. The workbench shown is made from maple and birch-veneer plywood.

Plane the 8/4 stock to 1³/₄ inches thick and cut the top braces, legs, and feet. Set some 1³/₄-inch-thick

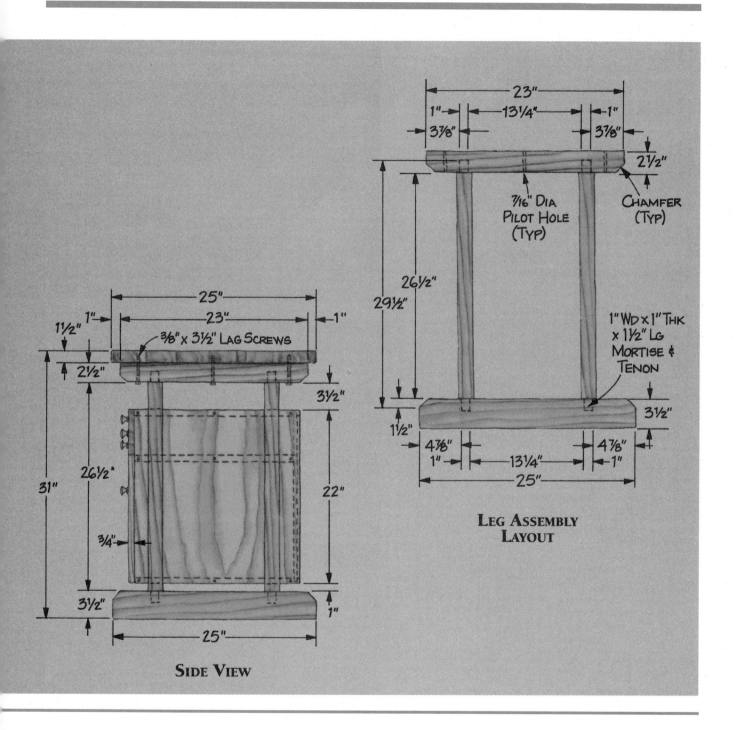

SIDE VIEW

LEG ASSEMBLY LAYOUT

stock aside to use as test pieces, then plane the remaining stock to 1½ inches thick. Cut this into 1½-inch-wide strips. Glue these strips edge to edge to make the benchtop. Be sure to orient these strips so the annual rings run top to bottom, as shown on page 9. This will reduce the amount of swelling and shrinking across the width of the bench.

Plane the 4/4 stock to ¾ inch thick and cut the rails, stiles, and drawer faces. Set some of the ¾-inch-thick stock aside to use as test pieces, then plane the remaining stock to ½ inch thick. Cut the drawer guides, fronts, backs, and sides.

Finally, cut the plywood parts to size. Clearly label all the parts as you cut them.

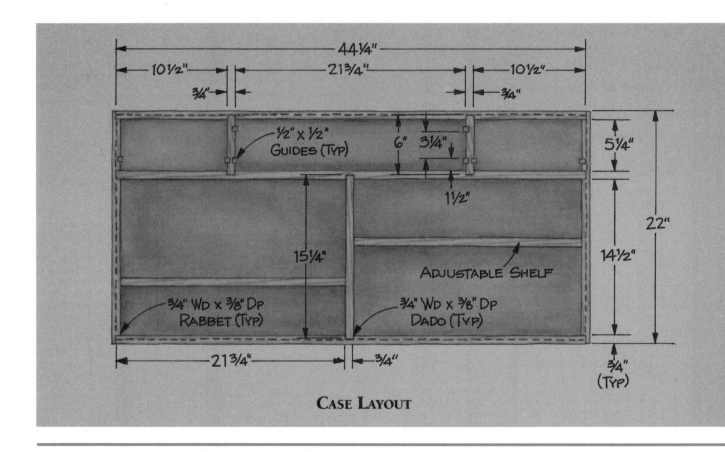

CASE LAYOUT

2 Cut the mortises and tenons in the top braces, legs, and feet. The top braces, legs, and feet form two frames which support the benchtop, as shown in the *Side View* and the *Leg Assembly Layout.* Tenons on the ends of the legs fit mortises in the feet and top braces. Cut the 1-inch-square, 1½-inch-deep mortises first, then cut the tenons to fit them. Refer to Chapter 5 for instructions on how to make mortise-and-tenon joints.

3 Chamfer the ends of the top braces and feet. As shown in the *Side View* and the *Leg Assembly Layout,* the top corners of the feet and the bottom corners of the top braces are chamfered. Cut these chamfers on a table saw or a band saw.

4 Drill pilot holes in the top braces. The benchtop is secured to the leg assemblies with lag screws. Drill ⁷⁄₁₆-inch-diameter pilot holes for these screws through the top braces, as shown in the *Leg Assembly Layout.* The precise location of these screws is not critical, but there should be at least three of them in each brace, and they should be evenly spaced along the length.

5 Assemble the legs, top braces, and feet. Dry assemble (*without* glue) the legs, top braces, and feet to be sure the mortise-and-tenon joints fit properly. When you're satisfied they do, finish sand the parts. Reassemble the parts with glue, let the glue dry, then sand all the surfaces clean and flush.

6 Cut the rabbets and dadoes in the plywood case parts. The cabinet case is a large plywood box held together with simple rabbets, dadoes, and grooves. Cut these joints:

■ ³⁄₄-inch-wide, ³⁄₈-inch-deep rabbets in the top and bottom edges of the case sides, as shown in the *Case Side Layout,* to hold the case top and bottom

■ ³⁄₄-inch-wide, ³⁄₈-inch-deep dado in the case sides to hold the case shelf

■ ³⁄₄-inch-wide, ³⁄₈-inch-deep dadoes in the case top, bottom, and fixed shelf, as shown in the *Case Layout,* to hold the drawer dividers and cupboard divider

■ ½-inch-wide, ¼-inch-deep dadoes in the case sides to hold the drawer guides

■ ½-inch-wide, ¼-inch-deep grooves in the drawer dividers, as shown in the *Drawer Divider Layout,* to hold the drawer guides

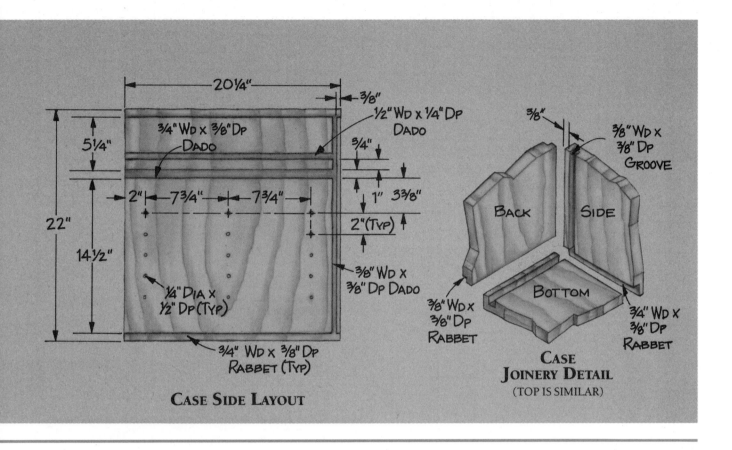

CASE SIDE LAYOUT

CASE JOINERY DETAIL
(TOP IS SIMILAR)

■ ³⁄₈-inch-wide, ³⁄₈-inch-deep grooves near the back edges of the case sides, top, and bottom, as shown in the *Case Joinery Detail,* to hold the case back

■ ³⁄₈-inch-wide, ³⁄₈-inch-deep rabbets in the edges of the case back to fit the grooves in the case sides, top, and bottom

7 Drill holes in the case sides and cupboard divider.   The adjustable shelves rest on support pins. These pins fit into holes inside the case. Drill ¹⁄₄-inch-diameter, ¹⁄₂-inch-deep holes in the case sides, as shown in the *Case Side Layout,* and ¹⁄₄-inch-diameter holes through the cupboard divider, as shown in the *Cupboard Divider Layout.*

8 Attach the drawer guides to the sides and dividers.   The drawers slide in and out of the case on drawer guides — hardwood strips inlaid in the plywood. Sand the drawer guides smooth, then glue them in the ¹⁄₂-inch-wide dadoes and grooves in the case sides and drawer dividers.

9 Assemble the case.   Finish sand all the plywood parts you've made so far. Assemble the fixed shelf, drawer dividers, and cupboard divider with glue and #8 x 1¹⁄₄-inch flathead wood screws. Countersink the heads of the screws flush with the surface of the wood. Let the glue set.

Lay the back, rear-side down, on a work surface. Place the divider assembly on top of it. Attach the case sides, top, and bottom to the back and divider assembly with glue and screws. Counterbore *and* countersink the screws, then cover the screw heads with plugs. Let the glue dry and sand all joints and plugs flush with the plywood surface. Be careful not to sand through the veneer.

10 Assemble the workbench.   Finish sand the benchtop. Attach the case to the leg assemblies, driving #12 x 2-inch flathead wood screws through the case from the *inside* and into the legs. Use three screws for each leg, and space them evenly along the length of the leg. Fasten the benchtop to the leg assemblies by driving lag screws up through the top braces and into the underside of the benchtop.

11 Cut the mortises and tenons in the door rails and stiles.   The rails and stiles on the frame-

and-panel doors are joined with haunched mortises and tenons. Cut ¼-inch-wide, ⅜-inch-deep grooves in the inside edges of all the door rails and stiles, as shown in the *Door Frame Joinery Detail*. Then cut ¼-inch-wide, 1¼-inch-long, 1¼-inch-deep mortises near both ends of each stile. Cut ¼-inch-thick, 1¼-inch-long tenons in the ends of the rails, then make a notch or "haunch" in the outer corner of each tenon to fit the mortise and groove in the stile. See page 75 for complete instructions on how to make a haunched mortise-and-tenon joint.

12 Assemble the doors. Finish sand the door parts, then assemble the rails and stiles with glue. As you fit the rails and stiles together, slide the panels into the grooves. However, *don't* glue the panels in place. Let them float in the grooves.

13 Hang the doors. The doors on the workbench swing on self-closing European-style hinges. These cabinet hinges offer several advantages over traditional butt hinges. They are much easier to install; you don't have to cut hinge mortises. They allow you to adjust the positions of the doors slightly even *after* you hang them. And they keep the doors closed without having to use an additional catch.

Mark the locations of the hinges on the case and door frames. Drill 1⅜-inch-diameter holes in the door frame stiles to mount the body of each hinge. Attach the hinges to the case and doors with screws, then adjust the position of the doors to open and shut without binding. The doors should completely cover the front edges of the case bottom and case shelf, and the outside edges of the end doors should be flush with the case sides. (SEE FIGURES 10-1 AND 10-2.)

Shut the door and mark the location of the door pulls. Drill pilot holes in the stiles and install the pulls.

14 Cut the drawer joinery. Like the case, the drawers are assembled with simple rabbets, dadoes, and grooves. Cut these joints:

■ ⁹⁄₁₆-inch-wide, ¼-inch-deep grooves in the outside faces of the drawer sides to fit the drawer guides

■ ½-inch-wide, ¼-inch-deep rabbets in the inside front ends of the drawer sides to hold the drawer fronts

■ ½-inch-wide, ¼-inch-deep dadoes in the inside faces of the drawer sides, near the back ends, to hold the drawer backs

■ ¼-inch-wide, ¼-inch-deep grooves in the inside faces of the drawer fronts, backs, and sides, near the bottom edges, to hold the drawer bottoms

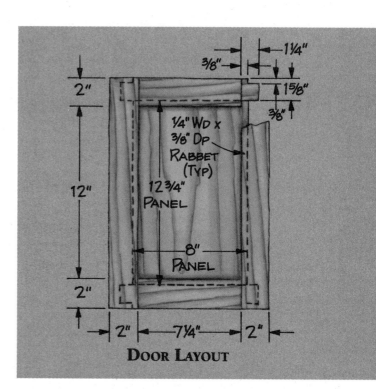

DOOR LAYOUT

10-1 Using a large piloted Forstner bit, drill 1⅜-inch-diameter, ½-inch-deep holes in the door stiles to house the hinge bodies. These drill bits are available from most mail-order woodworking suppliers or any hardware dealer that sells European-style cabinet hinges.

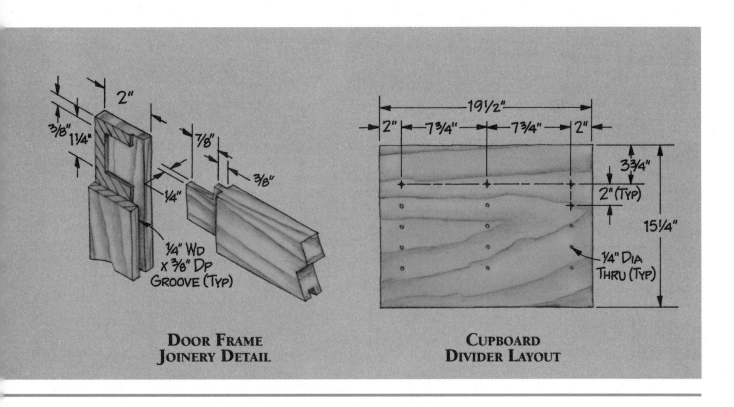

**DOOR FRAME
JOINERY DETAIL**

**CUPBOARD
DIVIDER LAYOUT**

10-2 Use a template and a spring-
loaded Vix bit to locate and bore the
pilot holes for the screws that will
hold the hinges to the case. (The Vix
bit automatically centers small pilot
holes inside the larger holes in the
template.) Both the template and the
bit are available from the same suppliers that offer the hinges.

15 Assemble and fit the drawers.   Finish sand
the parts of the drawers. Glue the sides, fronts, and
backs together. Slide the bottoms into place as you
assemble the other parts, but do *not* glue them in
their grooves. Let them float. When the glue dries,
reinforce the rabbet joints that hold the sides to the
fronts with 1-inch brads. Sand all joints clean and
flush.

Test the fit of the drawers in the case. The grooves
in the sides should fit smoothly over the drawer
guides, and the drawers should slide in and out of the
case without binding. If a drawer sticks, inspect it
carefully to determine which parts are rubbing. Plane
a little stock off the offending part of the drawer and
try again. Continue until all the drawers fit properly.

TRY THIS TRICK

If you have trouble deciding which drawer
part is binding inside the case, lightly rub some
chalk on the surfaces of the assembled drawer.
Slide the drawer into place, then pull it out again.
Inspect the inside of the case for chalk — this will
tell you which part of the drawer is rubbing and
where.

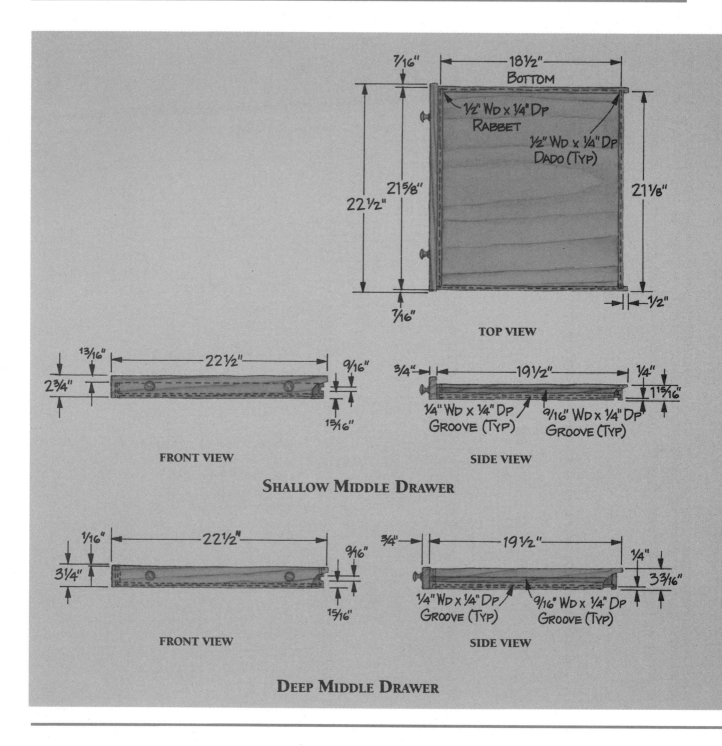

7/16" ←—— 18½" ——→
         BOTTOM

½" WD x ¼" DP
RABBET

½" WD x ¼" DP
DADO (TYP)

22½"   21⅝"   21⅛"

7/16"   ½"

TOP VIEW

13/16" ←——— 22½" ———→ 9/16"
2¾"   15/16"

FRONT VIEW

¾" ←——— 19½" ———→ ¼"
                                    1⁵⁄₁₆"
¼" WD x ¼" DP   9/16" WD x ¼" DP
GROOVE (TYP)   GROOVE (TYP)

SIDE VIEW

SHALLOW MIDDLE DRAWER

1/16" ←——— 22½" ———→ 9/16"
3¼"   15/16"

FRONT VIEW

¾" ←——— 19½" ———→ ¼"
                                    3³⁄₁₆"
¼" WD x ¼" DP   9/16" WD x ¼" DP
GROOVE (TYP)   GROOVE (TYP)

SIDE VIEW

DEEP MIDDLE DRAWER

16 Attach the drawer faces. Slide the drawers into place in the case. Mark the locations of the pulls on the drawer faces and drill pilot holes for them. Finish sand the drawer fronts.

Hold each drawer face in place over the appropriate drawer front. Use the pilot holes in the face as guides to drill pilot holes through the drawer front. Apply glue to the drawer front, then secure the face to the front. To hold the face while the glue dries, drive a screw through the pilot holes. Let the glue dry, then remove the screws and attach the pulls.

If the drawer fronts rub on one another — or on the doors — as you slide the drawers in and out of the cabinet, remove a little stock from the appropriate

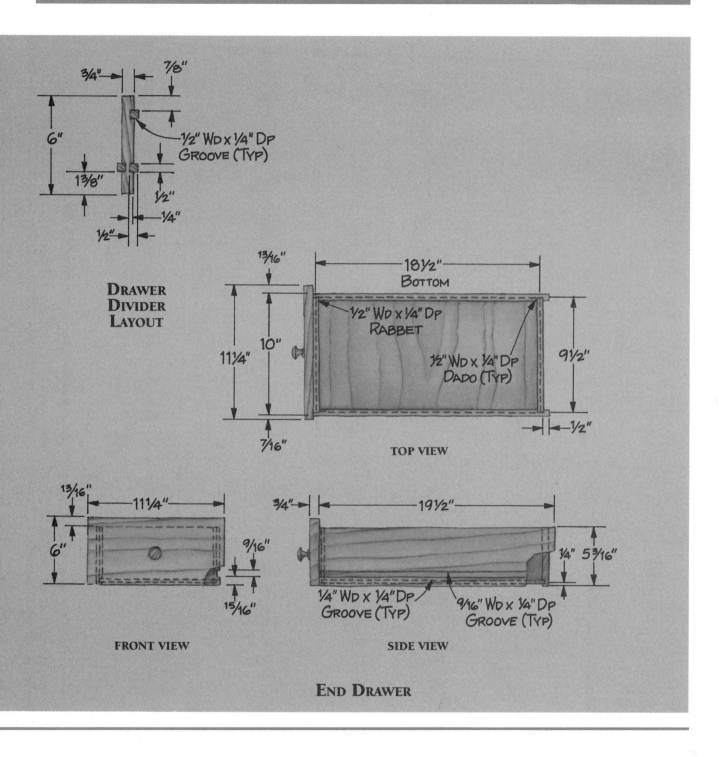

DRAWER DIVIDER LAYOUT

3/4" 7/8"

6"

1 3/8"

1/2"

1/4"

1/2"

1/2" WD x 1/4" DP GROOVE (TYP)

13/16"

18 1/2"
BOTTOM

1/2" WD x 1/4" DP RABBET

1/2" WD x 1/4" DP DADO (TYP)

10"

11 1/4"

9 1/2"

1/2"

7/16"

TOP VIEW

13/16"

11 1/4"

6"

9/16"

15/16"

FRONT VIEW

3/4"

19 1/2"

1/4" WD x 1/4" DP GROOVE (TYP)

9/16" WD x 1/4" DP GROOVE (TYP)

1/4" 5 3/16"

SIDE VIEW

END DRAWER

edge with a hand plane. When all the drawer fronts are installed, they should completely cover the front edges of the case, and their edges should be even with the top and sides of the case.

17 Finish the workbench. Remove the doors and drawers from the case, and remove the hardware from the doors and drawers. Do any necessary touch-up sanding, then apply a finish to *all* wooden surfaces, inside and out. Use a penetrating finish that will be easy to repair, such as tung oil or Danish oil. Wax and buff the outside surfaces. Apply at least two coats of wax to the benchtop — this will help prevent glue from sticking to the surface.

INDEX

Note: Page references in *italic* indicate photograph or illustration numbers. **Boldface** references indicate charts or tables.

WOODWORKING GLOSSARY

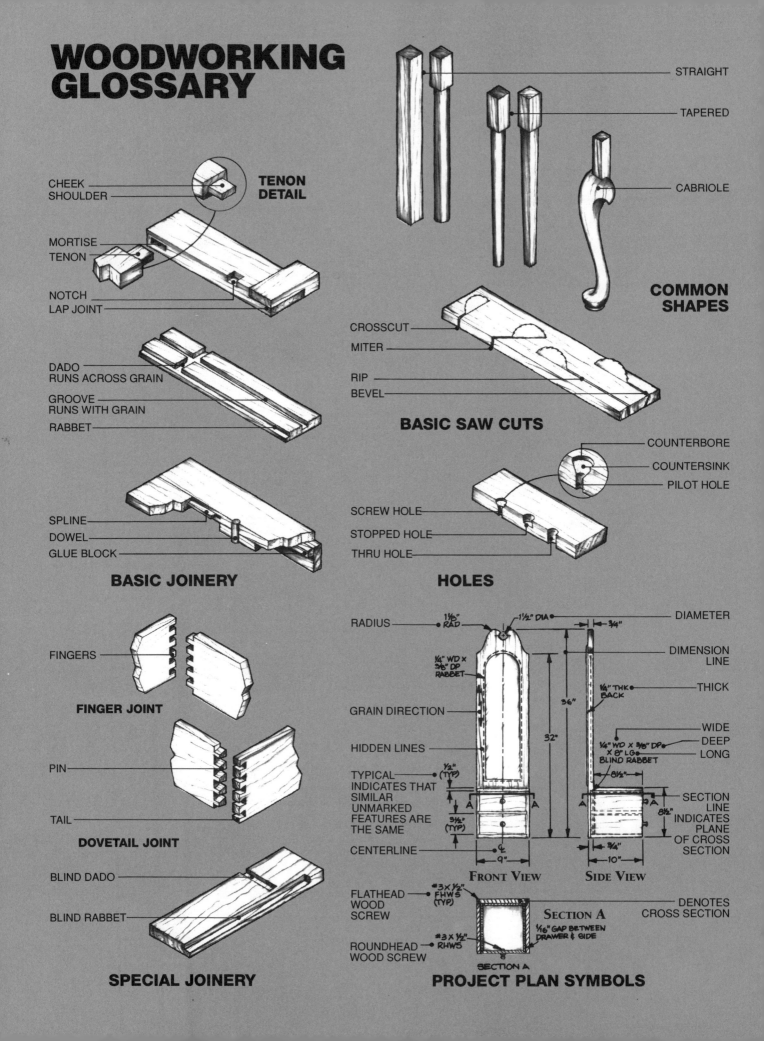

TENON DETAIL
CHEEK
SHOULDER

MORTISE
TENON
NOTCH
LAP JOINT

DADO RUNS ACROSS GRAIN
GROOVE RUNS WITH GRAIN
RABBET

SPLINE
DOWEL
GLUE BLOCK

BASIC JOINERY

FINGERS

FINGER JOINT

PIN
TAIL

DOVETAIL JOINT

BLIND DADO
BLIND RABBET

SPECIAL JOINERY

STRAIGHT
TAPERED
CABRIOLE

COMMON SHAPES

CROSSCUT
MITER
RIP
BEVEL

BASIC SAW CUTS

COUNTERBORE
COUNTERSINK
PILOT HOLE

SCREW HOLE
STOPPED HOLE
THRU HOLE

HOLES

RADIUS — 1⅛" RAD
1½" DIA — DIAMETER
¾"
¼" WD X ⅜" DP RABBET
DIMENSION LINE
¼" THK BACK — THICK
36"
32"
GRAIN DIRECTION
WIDE
¼" WD X ⅜" DP X 8" LG BLIND RABBET — DEEP / LONG
HIDDEN LINES
8½"
TYPICAL INDICATES THAT SIMILAR UNMARKED FEATURES ARE THE SAME — ½" (TYP)
A
A
3½" (TYP)
8½"
SECTION LINE INDICATES PLANE OF CROSS SECTION
CENTERLINE — ₵
¾"
9"
10"
FRONT VIEW   **SIDE VIEW**

FLATHEAD WOOD SCREW — #3 X ½" FHWS (TYP)
SECTION A
DENOTES CROSS SECTION
1/16" GAP BETWEEN DRAWER & SIDE
ROUNDHEAD WOOD SCREW — #3 X ½" RHWS
SECTION A

PROJECT PLAN SYMBOLS